Desire2Learn for Higher Education Cookbook

Gain expert knowledge of the tools within the Desire2Learn Learning Environment, maximize your productivity, and create online learning experiences with these easy-to-follow recipes

Brandon Ballentine

BIRMINGHAM - MUMBAI

Desire2Learn for Higher Education Cookbook

First published: November, 2012

Production Reference: 1161112

Published by Packt Publishing Ltd.
Livery Place
35 Livery Street
Birmingham B3 2PB, UK.

ISBN 978-1-84969-344-8

www.packtpub.com

Cover Image by Duraid Fatouhi (duraidfatouhi@yahoo.com)

Credits

Author
Brandon Ballentine

Reviewers
Susan Smith Nash

Chris Scharlach

Acquisition Editor
Joanna Finchen

Lead Technical Editor
Arun Nadar

Technical Editor
Lubna Shaikh

Copy Editor
Alfida Paiva

Project Coordinator
Vishal Bodwani

Proofreaders
Aaron Nash

Maria Gould

Elinor Perry Smith

Indexer
Tejal Daruwale

Production Coordinator
Conidon Miranda

Cover Work
Conidon Miranda

About the Author

Brandon Ballentine is an Instructional Technologist in East Tennessee. He is a D2L system administrator and provides faculty training on D2L and other educational tools. Brandon also teaches workshops on iOS Application Development and Mobile Web Design.

Prior to working in the educational technology field, Brandon developed and managed interactive technologies for a financial institution.

Brandon has a Master's degree in English from East Tennessee State University. In his free time, he enjoys travelling and photography. To learn more about Brandon and his latest projects, visit www.brandonballentine.com.

I would like to thank my wife Lia for her patience and support during the writing of this book.

About the Reviewer

Susan Smith Nash is the author of several books on e-learning, including *Moodle 1.9 Teaching Techniques*. Nash has reviewed several Packt Publishing books, including the *JavaScript Cookbook* and *Moodle Security*. Nash has developed and administered online learning programs since the 1990s, and is the publisher of an edublog, E-Learning Queen. Having obtained her Ph.D. from the University of Oklahoma, Susan lives in Norman, Oklahoma, where she enjoys tennis, running, writing experimental fiction, and reading texts on the philosophy of technology.

www.PacktPub.com

Support files, eBooks, discount offers and more

You might want to visit www.PacktPub.com for support files and downloads related to your book.

Did you know that Packt offers eBook versions of every book published, with PDF and ePub files available? You can upgrade to the eBook version at www.PacktPub.com and as a print book customer, you are entitled to a discount on the eBook copy. Get in touch with us at service@packtpub.com for more details.

At www.PacktPub.com, you can also read a collection of free technical articles, sign up for a range of free newsletters and receive exclusive discounts and offers on Packt books and eBooks.

http://PacktLib.PacktPub.com

Do you need instant solutions to your IT questions? PacktLib is Packt's online digital book library. Here, you can access, read and search across Packt's entire library of books.

Why Subscribe?

- Fully searchable across every book published by Packt
- Copy and paste, print and bookmark content
- On demand and accessible via web browser

Free Access for Packt account holders

If you have an account with Packt at www.PacktPub.com, you can use this to access PacktLib today and view nine entirely free books. Simply use your login credentials for immediate access.

Table of Contents

Preface

Creating an engaging online or web-enhanced class in the Desire2Learn Learning Environment doesn't have to be difficult. The easy-to-follow recipes in this cookbook guide you through everything from getting your course ready for students to calculating final grades.

Desire2Learn for Higher Education Cookbook offers recipes that will help you set up, customize, and conduct your online courses, whether you're new to the system or a seasoned D2L user. The recipes are written for version 10.0 of the learning suite, although many of the examples are also applicable for version 9.4.

The cookbook is organized around tasks that instructors address during a typical semester, starting with a basic course setup and working towards calculating final grades.

Early recipes focus on creating a personalized learning environment by helping you customize the look and feel of your course and its content. Other recipes in the cookbook teach you how to integrate your favorite multimedia and social networking sites. Later chapters offer recipes for productivity in several of the learning environment's tools.

Desire2Learn for Higher Education Cookbook is filled with screenshots and detailed steps to increase your productivity when working in the learning environment, to create and facilitate your online courses.

What this book covers

Chapter 1, Getting Your Course Ready for a New Semester, focuses on the essential beginning-of-the-semester tasks, such as copying materials from one course to another, modifying assignment due dates, and previewing your course from a student's point of view.

Chapter 2, Personalizing Your Course, focuses on how to modify a course's navbar and theme to achieve a unique look and feel. Readers will also learn how to use system variables to display custom content to students.

Chapter 3, Getting Materials into Your Course, presents a collection of time-saving tips for adding content to your course, whether it's a Google Document, material from the Learning Object Repository, or a `.zip` folder.

Chapter 4, Working with Multimedia, is all about locating and adding videos to your course.

Chapter 5, Diving into HTML Code, explores ways you can use HTML and CSS to create content that looks great on a variety of screen sizes.

Chapter 6, Managing Assessments, discusses solutions to common issues instructors face throughout the semester. In addition, readers will learn how to speed up the quiz creation process and minimize cheating in online assessments.

Chapter 7, Collaboration and Participation, focuses on how you can use system tools and external web services to encourage and monitor participation in your course.

Chapter 8, Working with the Grades Tool, presents a variety of tips for making the most out of the Learning Environment's Grades tool, such as how to set up the tool to minimize scrolling and how to export a backup copy of the grade book for safe keeping.

What you need for this book

You will need access to a Desire2Learn Learning Environment course and a modern web browser. Some recipes require additional software tools such as Microsoft Office, or accounts on various Web services such as YouTube.

Who this book is for

If you're familiar with the system's basic tools but want to do more with your course, then this book is for you.

Conventions

In this book, you will find a number of styles of text that distinguish between different kinds of information. Here are some examples of these styles, and an explanation of their meaning.

Code words in text are shown as follows: "Replacing `your-school.edu` with the actual URL for your organization's Desire2Learn instance."

New terms and **important words** are shown in bold. Words that you see on the screen, in menus or dialog boxes for example, appear in the text like this: "Start by accessing the destination course from **My Homepage**.".

Reader feedback

Feedback from our readers is always welcome. Let us know what you think about this book—what you liked or may have disliked. Reader feedback is important for us to develop titles that you really get the most out of.

To send us general feedback, simply send an e-mail to `feedback@packtpub.com`, and mention the book title via the subject of your message.

If there is a book that you need and would like to see us publish, please send us a note in the **SUGGEST A TITLE** form on `www.packtpub.com` or e-mail `suggest@packtpub.com`.

If there is a topic that you have expertise in and you are interested in either writing or contributing to a book, see our author guide on `www.packtpub.com/authors`.

Customer support

Now that you are the proud owner of a Packt book, we have a number of things to help you to get the most from your purchase.

Errata

Although we have taken every care to ensure the accuracy of our content, mistakes do happen. If you find a mistake in one of our books—maybe a mistake in the text or the code—we would be grateful if you would report this to us. By doing so, you can save other readers from frustration and help us improve subsequent versions of this book. If you find any errata, please report them by visiting `http://www.packtpub.com/support`, selecting your book, clicking on the **errata submission form** link, and entering the details of your errata. Once your errata are verified, your submission will be accepted and the errata will be uploaded on our website, or added to any list of existing errata, under the Errata section of that title. Any existing errata can be viewed by selecting your title from `http://www.packtpub.com/support`.

Piracy

Piracy of copyright material on the Internet is an ongoing problem across all media. At Packt, we take the protection of our copyright and licenses very seriously. If you come across any illegal copies of our works, in any form, on the Internet, please provide us with the location address or website name immediately so that we can pursue a remedy.

Please contact us at `copyright@packtpub.com` with a link to the suspected pirated material.

We appreciate your help in protecting our authors, and our ability to bring you valuable content.

Questions

You can contact us at `questions@packtpub.com` if you are having a problem with any aspect of the book, and we will do our best to address it.

1
Getting Your Course Ready for a New Semester

In this chapter, we will cover the following recipes:

- ▸ Copying course materials from a previous semester
- ▸ Importing a publisher's course cartridge
- ▸ Changing many due dates from one screen
- ▸ Double-checking everything from the student view
- ▸ Configuring your web browser

Introduction

Getting your course ready for students at the beginning of each semester can be a daunting task. You'll need to verify links to external content, make sure that previous materials have been copied successfully to your new course, and modify the existing assignment dates, among other tasks. You get the point—there are quite a few things you need to take care of before students ever see your course. This chapter offers recipes for streamlining this process to make setting up your course as stress-free as possible.

The first two recipes deal with getting materials into your course, whether you're copying an entire course from a previous semester or importing a compatible course cartridge provided by a textbook publisher. You may be surprised to know that course cartridges created for other **Learning Management Systems** (**LMSs**), such as Blackboard and Moodle, can often be imported without any trouble! Other recipes in the chapter focus on making quick work of date changes and external link validation. We'll wrap up the chapter by previewing everything from the student's view.

Please note that the recipes in this chapter, as well as the rest of the book, are written for Version 10.0 of the **Desire2Learn Learning Environment**. While many of the recipes are also applicable to earlier versions of the system, you may need to modify the steps to follow along.

Copying course materials from a previous semester

Copying materials, activities, and settings from one course to another can save you a considerable amount of time when preparing for the start of a new semester. The learning environment's **Import/Export/Copy Components** tool allows you to easily clone an entire course or select just the parts of the original course that you want to use in a new course. In this recipe, we will discuss copying materials from an existing course within the system. We will use the same tool to import a course cartridge from a publisher in the next recipe.

Getting ready

The **Desire2Learn** (**D2L**) Learning Environment is highly customizable, and each organization that uses it can customize many aspects of the user experience. This recipe assumes that your school has allowed the use of the Import/Export/Copy Components tool for your specific role within the system. In order to complete this recipe, you'll also need access to two courses—an empty course that we will be copying materials to and another one that contains the materials we will be copying. To copy materials from one course to another, your role in both courses needs to allow the use of the **Copy Components** function. For example, you wouldn't be able to copy quizzes from a class in which you are enrolled as a student into one that you are teaching.

How to do it...

We will be working with two courses in this recipe – a new, empty course and an existing course that contains the materials to be copied. Remember to start by accessing the destination course or the course that you want to copy materials to.

1. Start by accessing the destination course from **My Homepage**.
2. Click on the **Edit Course** link in the course navigation bar.
3. Click the **Import/Export/Copy Components** link under the **Site Resources** heading.
4. Select the option **Copy Components from Another Org Unit** and then click on **Start**.

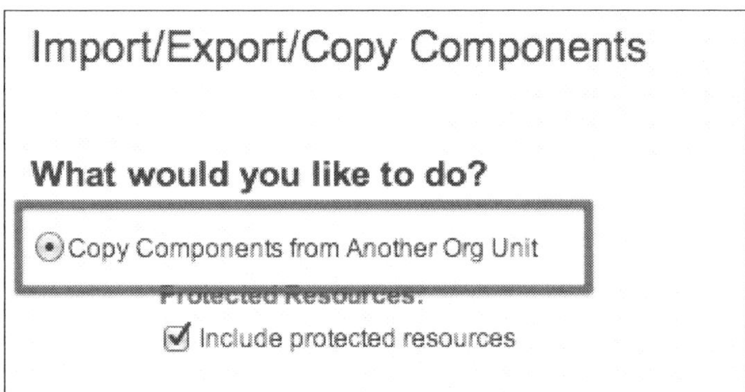

5. Locate the course from which we will be copying materials by clicking on the **Search for offering** link. If needed, use the search tool at the top of the list of courses to help locate the course. You can also click on any of the column headers to sort the list of courses based on that field (clicking twice reverses the order). Check the radio button to the left of the course, and click on the **Add Selected** button.

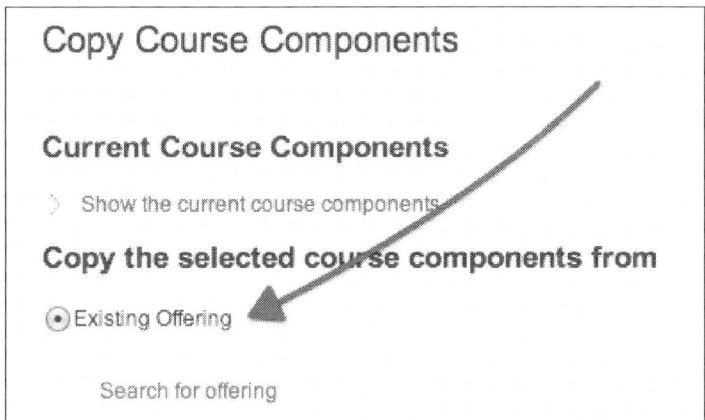

6. Within a few seconds, the page updates to display all of the available components from the course we just selected. To clone an entire course, check the **Select All Components** box, and click on the **Continue** button.

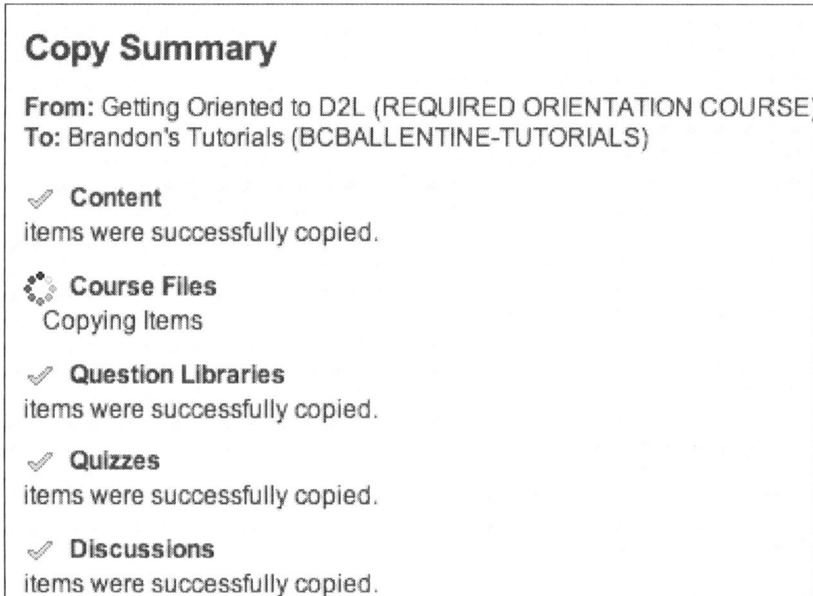

7. Since we chose to clone an entire course, we can continue on our way by clicking on the **Finish** button.

8. Depending on the amount of materials being copied and the server load, the copy process may take a few seconds to several minutes. When the **Done** button becomes active, it means that the process has completed. As each tool finishes copying, you'll see its progress indicator change into a green checkmark. Anything that didn't copy successfully will be noted in the summary.

How it works...

We start off by accessing the destination course. The **Search for Offering** screen displays a list of all of the courses you currently have access to copy from. If you've been teaching for a while, this list may be quite large. The search and filtering tools at the top of the course offering list may be helpful if you are having difficulty finding the correct course from the list.

Select Course Offering

Search For: [   ]   Search | Hide Search Options

Search In: ☑ Offering Name   ☑ Offering Code
             ☑ Department   ☑ Offering Path

Date and Time: ☐ The Beginning

                 3/24/2012   Now
                 United States - New York
             ☐ The End

                 3/31/2012   Now
                 United States - New York

In this recipe, we copied all the available components from the source offering by choosing the **Select All Components** option. However, you can copy individual tools or even individual items within those tools by choosing the **Select individual items to copy** option. If you decide to copy specific components, then you need to select those items on the **Choose Components to Copy** screen, as shown in the following screenshot:

Choose Components to Copy

☐ Select All Components
    ☑ **Calendar** (14 item(s))

        ◯ Copy all items
        ◉ Select individual items to copy
    ☐ **Checklists** (2 item(s))

        ◉ Copy all items
        ◯ Select individual items to copy
    ☑ **Content** (133 item(s))

        ◯ Copy all items
        ◉ Select individual items to copy

There's more...

If you're copying large course files or complex question libraries, there's a chance that your browser will time out before the copy process is complete. If this happens, there are a few things you can do to complete the task:

> ▸ Break up the copy process into several smaller jobs. If, for example, you're getting error messages while copying **Course Files**, try only copying half of the files, then return to the tool and try the second half later.

> ▸ The current server load can greatly impact the time it takes to copy components. You may want to try copying the components during an off-peak time.

> ▸ If you experience a browser time-out while copying **Course Files**, you might want to visit **File Manager** and look for duplicate or large files in the source course. Deleting unnecessary files can speed up the process significantly.

> ▸ Your Desire2Learn administrator has access to other ways of cloning a course or copying files. If you continue to experience difficulty with the tool, talking with your friendly admin would be a great idea!

Importing a publisher's course cartridge

Publishers frequently offer complimentary course cartridges to instructors who adopt their textbooks. The content of these cartridges varies greatly, but can include content and files, assessments, web links, and more. In this recipe, we will walk through the process of importing a course cartridge into an existing Desire2Learn Learning Environment course.

Getting ready

In order to complete this recipe, you'll need either a publisher's cartridge or an export from another Desire2Learn Learning Environment course. These files come in the form of `.zip` archives. Publishers typically offer different versions of cartridges for several of the major learning management systems. While you may not always find a version of a particular cartridge formatted for the Desire2Learn Learning Environment, you may be surprised to know that versions made for other systems, such as Blackboard 6 and WebCT, will typically work just fine. Check with your system administrator, if you have any difficulties importing a cartridge.

You will also need access to the Import/Export/Copy Components tool. You will need to talk with your Desire2Learn system administrator if your role in the current course does not include access to the tool.

How to do it...

1. Start off by accessing the destination course from the **My Home** page.

2. Click on the **Edit Course** link in the course's navigation bar.

3. Access the **Import/Export/Copy Components** tool by clicking on the link under the **Site Resources** heading.

4. Select the option to **Import Components**. Then, select the **from a File** option and choose the cartridge to import by clicking on the **Choose File** button. Click on the **Start** button after locating and selecting the file:

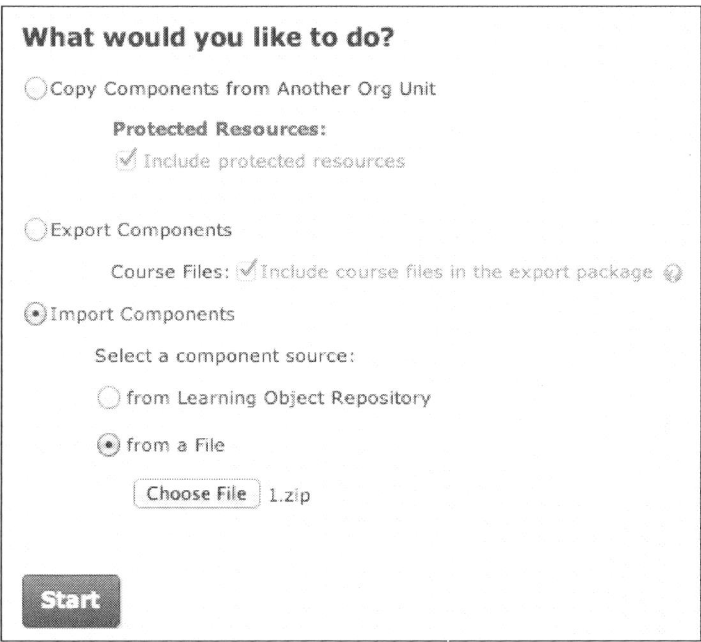

5. Click on the **Continue** button on the **Preprocessing** screen when it becomes available.

6. Import the entire cartridge's contents by choosing the **Select All Components** checkbox and then clicking on the **Continue** button.

7. Click on the **Continue** button on the **Confirm Import Selections** screen.

8. The process is complete when all of the progress indicators have changed to green checkmarks. Click on **Finish**, then **Done** when the components are finished copying.

How it works...

We start off by accessing the **Import/Export/Copy Components** tool in the destination course. After selecting the `.zip` folder to import, the system uploads and pre-processes the archive's `manifest` file. Depending on the complexity of the cartridge and the size of the archive, this can happen very quickly or it may take quite some time.

After the pre-process action is complete, we choose to import the entire cartridge into the course, just as we did in the previous recipe. While this is often the easiest approach, it is possible to pick and choose individual components (such as Quizzes or Grades) or even individual items (such as specific quizzes or grade items), as we will discuss in the following section.

Once you verify the components to be imported, it's just a matter of waiting for the progress indicators to become green checkmarks. Any item not able to be imported will be displayed on screen at the end of the process. You probably won't run into too many problems unless you are importing extremely large or complex cartridges, but it is always a good idea to verify that everything was successful before clicking on the **Done** button.

There's more...

In the last two scenarios, we have seen examples of copying and importing entire courses. While this is common at the beginning of the semester, there may be times when you will need only certain parts of another course. Suppose, for example, you only want the question library portion of a publisher's course cartridge. Luckily, this is easily accomplished by selecting individual components on the **Choose Components to Copy** screen instead of the **All Components** option.

In the following screenshot, I have chosen to copy all the available **Content** items, but only selected **Discussions** and **Dropbox** folders:

Choose Components to Copy

☐ Select All Components

☑ **Content** (2 item(s))

    ◉ Copy all items

    ○ Select individual items to copy

☐ **Content Display Settings**

    ◉ Copy all items

☑ **Course Files** (1 item(s))

    ◉ Copy all items

    ○ Select individual items to copy

☑ **Discussions** (2 item(s))

    ○ Copy all items

    ◉ Select individual items to copy

☑ **Dropbox** (1 item(s))

    ○ Copy all items

    ◉ Select individual items to copy

After selecting the components to copy and clicking on the **Continue** button, I'm prompted to select the individual quizzes I want to copy into my course. Clicking on the **Expand All** link shows a list of all quizzes, and selecting individual items to be imported is as easy as checking the option next to the item titles. Since I've chosen to also import selected **Dropbox** folders, I would complete a similar process for selecting those items on the next screen:

Select Quizzes to Copy

☐ Select All

Expand All Collapse All

⊟ Quizzes without category

    ☐ Final Exam

    ☐ Syllabus Quiz

    ☑ Unit 1 Quiz

    ☑ Unit 2 Quiz

    ☑ Unit 3 Quiz

    ☑ Unit 4 Quiz

[Continue] [Go Back] [Cancel]

I should point out one "gotcha" that frequently causes trouble for new users of the Desire2Learn Learning Environment. Items under the **Content** heading are frequently linked to uploaded documents or system-generated HTML files, which are stored in the **File Manager**. Unfortunately, selecting the items under **Content** doesn't copy these associated files, so you need to manually select these files under **Course Files**. Since this can be a somewhat tricky task depending on how you've organized your files, you may find it easier to copy everything and delete what you do not need.

See also

▶ The *Copying course materials from a previous semester* recipe

Changing many due dates from one screen

There's a pretty good chance that you'll need to update quite a few assignments' start and end dates if you've populated your course by copying or importing materials from a previous semester. In earlier versions of the Learning Environment, this meant accessing each tool and editing each item whose date needed to be adjusted. Luckily, that's no longer the case—now we can quickly create, edit, or delete all items from one location. In this recipe, we will use the **Manage Dates** tool to change the due dates for all dropbox folders in an example course.

Getting ready

To complete this recipe, you'll need a course with some date-restricted materials or activities. We will be adjusting the dates of dropbox folders in this example, but feel free to edit whatever you like.

How to do it...

1. Access a course from the **My Home** page.
2. Click on the **Edit Course** link in the course's navigation bar.
3. Click on the **Manage Dates** link under the **Site Resources** heading.
4. Let's start by updating all the dropbox due dates from the previous semester. Under **Filter Options**, select the option to search for **Specific Tools**. Then, uncheck each tool except for **Dropbox**. Click on the **Apply Filter** button.

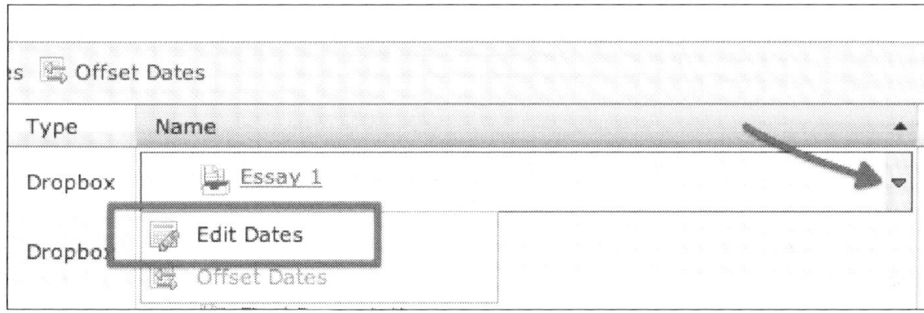

5. Click on the **Start Date** column header to sort the listings in chronological order.

6. Hover over the name of a quiz to reveal the contextual menu bar. Click on the small triangle icon and choose the **Edit Dates** option.

7. Choose new start and end dates, then click on the **Save** button.

8. Repeat the process for all of the quizzes in the course.

How it works...

By default, the **Manage Dates** tool lists all content, dropbox folders, assessments, news items, discussions, and grades in one table. If your course doesn't have a lot of content, this is probably fine. However, as your course grows, you may find it easier to filter by specific tools. In this recipe, we are only interested in changing the due dates for dropbox folders at the moment, so we narrow our selection to include only those items.

You further refine your search by clicking on any of the column headers to sort the data by different parameters. In this recipe, we sorted the dropbox items by their start date, but you can even sort by the end date, item name, and so on. Clicking on a header a second time reverses the sort order.

Although we chose to edit the dates for each quiz separately, you may have noticed the **Edit Dates** icon at the top of the table. By checking the boxes next to multiple items and clicking on the **Edit Dates** button, you can assign the same date to multiple items. This is useful for changing the dates for an entire unit or module.

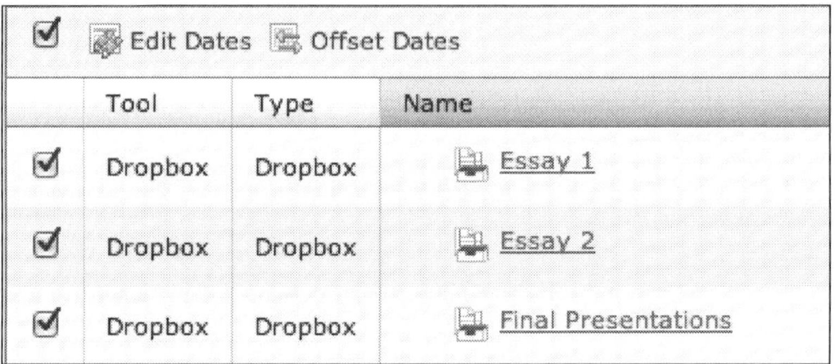

You may have also noticed the **Offset Dates** icon. This option is similar to the change dates function, but rather than setting specific dates, we move the existing dates either forward or backward a certain number of days. Although you could conceivably move the dates forward a whole semester, I find this option more useful for rearranging the schedule after college closings or class cancelations.

There's more...

The Manage Dates tool also gives you a quick way to entirely remove dates from items. Simply click on any of the red **X** icons to remove that date from the assignment.

The checkbox for the **Show in Calendar** option works in a similar way. Check the boxes for any item that you want to appear in the course.

See also

- The *Copying course materials from a previous semester* recipe

Double-checking everything from the student view

The Desire2Learn Learning Environment uses role-based permissions to control your experience within the system. We've seen this on the **My Home** page, where various system roles are presented by tabs above the list of available courses. Accessing a class in which you are enrolled as a student will be a much different experience compared to accessing one in which you are an instructor or developer. By the start of the semester, you've no doubt spent a lot of time getting everything in your course ready for student access. The problem is that you have been viewing everything from the instructor's point of view. Sometimes, however, seeing things from the student's perspective helps identify display or permission problems. It's good practice to double-check your course using the **Role Switch** tool before students gain access. In this recipe, we'll take a walk through our course, previewing everything from the student's perspective.

Getting ready

In order to complete this recipe, you need a Desire2Learn Learning Environment course and access to the **Role Switch** widget.

How to do it

1. Access a course from the **My Home** page.

2. Locate the **Role Switch** widget and select the **Student** role from the drop-down list. Click on the **Change Role** button.

3. Access the Content tool and try clicking on a few topics. Make sure that everything loads as expected.

4. Access the **Dropbox** tool and make sure that you are able to view all of the folders.

5. Go ahead and check out the other areas of the course as well. Come back here when you're finished.

6. Head back to the **Role Switch** widget and change your role back to normal. Make sure to click on the **Change Role** button after selecting a role from the drop-down list. We are going to do things a bit differently for the **Grades and Quizzes** tools.

7. Click on the **Quizzes** link in the course navigation bar. Click on and then click the **Preview** button. Take a look at the quiz and questions are formatted as expected. Feel free to exit the previ when you're done.

8. To wrap up this recipe, let's visit the Grades tool. Click on the r the students from the list of names on the **Enter Grades** page.

9. Click on the **Preview** link to simulate the student view in the **G**

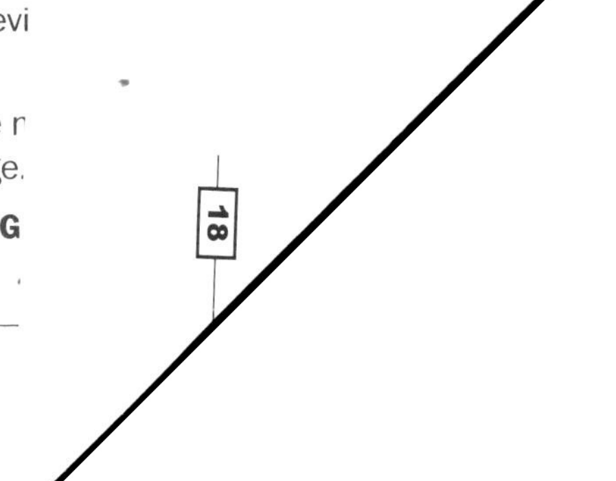

How it works

We make use of a few different tools in order to view everything in the course from the student's perspective. The **Role Switch** widget is a great way to check course news, checklists, content, and dropbox tools. While we can use it to view the list of course quizzes, we can't enter the quiz or grade book tools using that method. In order to access a quiz and view its questions, we need to use the **Preview** function of the quiz itself, as opposed to the **Role Switch** widget:

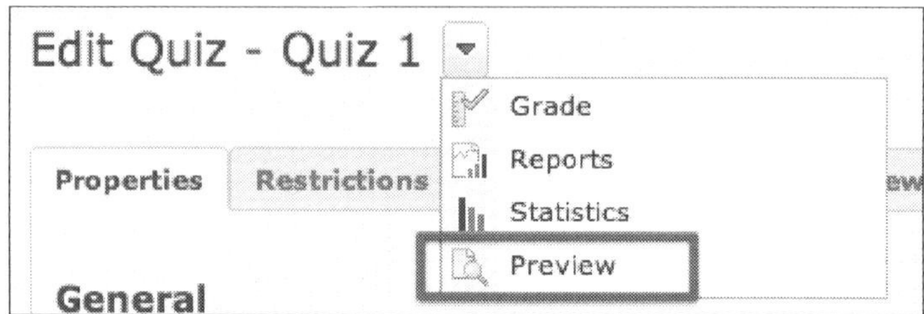

Similarly, to see what the grades tool looks like to students, we need to preview the tool for a particular student. Instructors normally aren't added to the grade book, therefore the **Role Switch** widget isn't really helpful in this case. Previewing the grade book for a student in the class will give us a much better idea of how everything looks.

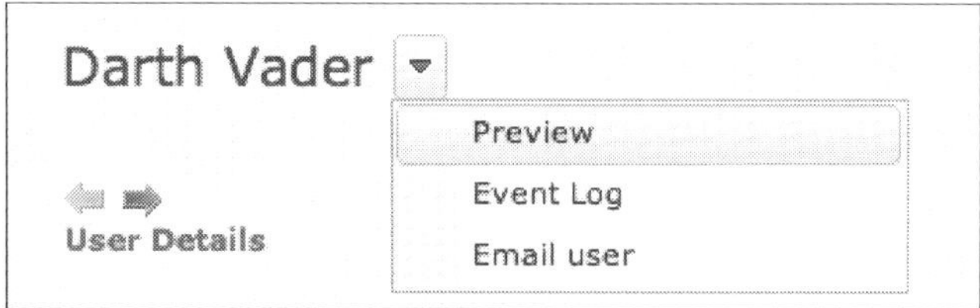

Configuring your web browser

Because the Desire2Learn Learning Environment is web-based, it's important to make sure you're using a web browser that's fully supported by the system and that you also have the appropriate plugins required to view certain types of content, such as Flash videos and Java applets. In this recipe, we will use the system's built-in **System Check** tool to make sure your browser is compliant. We will also learn how to set up Internet Explorer's security settings to avoid receiving those annoying "Navigation Canceled" messages that can create problems when displaying external content, such as YouTube videos.

How to do it

1. Launch the web browser that you plan on using to access your online courses.

2. Navigate to `https://your-school.edu/d2l/systemCheck`, replacing `your-school.edu` with the actual URL for your organization's Desire2Learn instance.

3. Make sure that you have all green checkmarks in both the **Critical System Checks** and **Non-critical System Checks** sections. If you see any recommendations, address those and then return to the System Check page to run the check again.

System Check

The following checks ensure that your browser is properly configured to use the system.

 **1 recommendation(s)**

Critical System Checks

✓ **JavaScript**
Pass - Your web browser supports JavaScript.

✓ **Cookies**
Pass - Cookies are enabled in your browser.

Non-critical System Checks

✓ **Browser**
Pass - Your browser is fully supported.

✓ **Flash**
Pass - Your browser has a compatible Adobe Flash plug-in.

✓ **Display**
Pass - Your screen resolution meets the recommended 1024 by 768 pixels.

⬇ **Java**
Recommendation - Your browser does not support Java.

✓ **Rich Content Editing**
Pass - Your browser supports rich content editing.

How it works...

Items in the **Critical System Checks** section are required to use the system. If your browser doesn't support JavaScript and cookies (or if you've turned them off), then you will not able to log in. While items in the **Non-critical System Checks** section are not required to log in, you may experience trouble viewing content or working within the system if you're using a non-supported browser or if your browser is missing recommended plugins.

The **System Check** page is a great starting point for making sure your browser is configured correctly, but you may need to adjust some other settings as well. For example, you will need to make sure your browser doesn't block pop ups, since the system uses them to display important information to users. You'll also need to verify that you have installed any other plugins required to view content in your course. I recommend keeping a list of required plugins in your course syllabus so that they can be easily accessed by both you and your students at the beginning of the semester.

If you're an Internet Explorer user, you may receive a "Navigation Canceled" message when attempting to view external content, such as web videos or social media widgets, embedded in a news or content item. This message is related to a security setting in IE where the browser is set to block non-secure content (from an HTTP address) from displaying on a secure page (HTTPS address). Normally, this is the type of behavior that you'd probably want. You don't, after all, want your bank's website to pull non-secure content into its secure online banking website. When we create quick links to external content or embed it in pages within the learning environment; however, this is exactly what we do want to allow, since most of these external websites are going to be hosted on non-secure (HTTP) servers.

In order to allow this type of behavior, we need to create an exception for our Desire2Learn site. We start by adding the server address to our list of **Trusted Sites**. We then adjust the settings of the trusted sites to allow for **Mixed Content**, or secure and non-secure content, to be displayed on the same webpage.

Once we save our changes, IE should have no issues presenting non-secure content within the Desire2Learn Learning Environment.

1. Open Internet Explorer.
2. In the **Tools** menu, choose **Internet Options**.
3. Access the **Security** tab.
4. Click on the **Trusted Sites** list and add your organization's D2L URL by clicking on the **Sites** button:

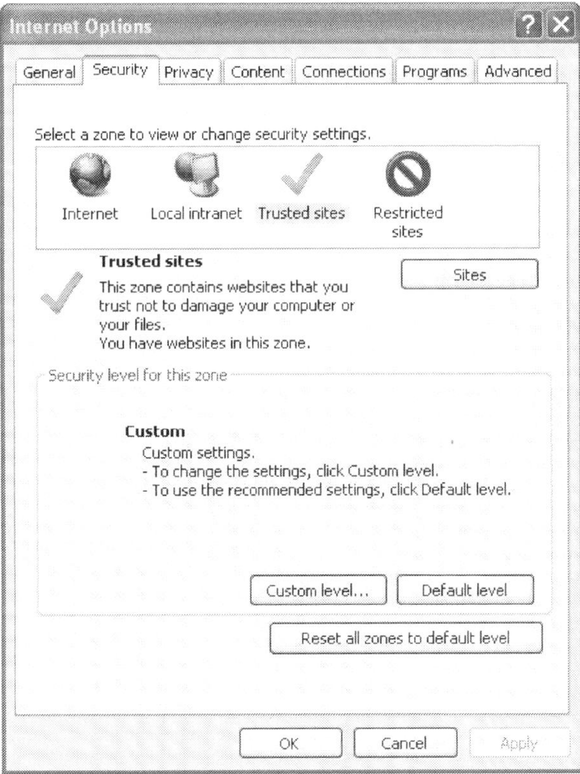

5. A little further down on the panel, click on the **Custom Level** button to assign a custom security level for **Trusted sites**.

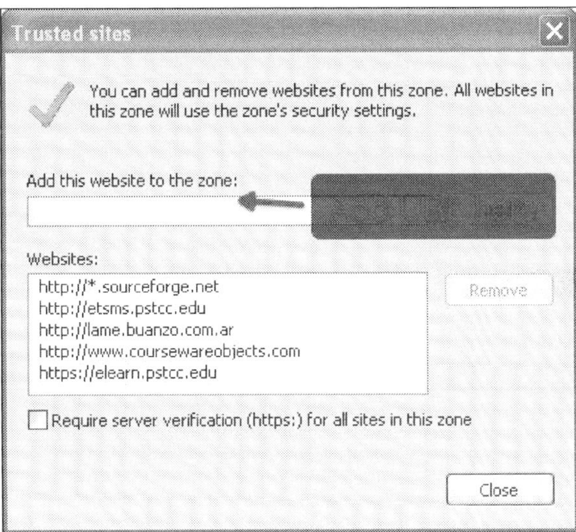

6. Locate the **Allow Mixed Content** heading, choose the **Enable** option, and click on **OK**:

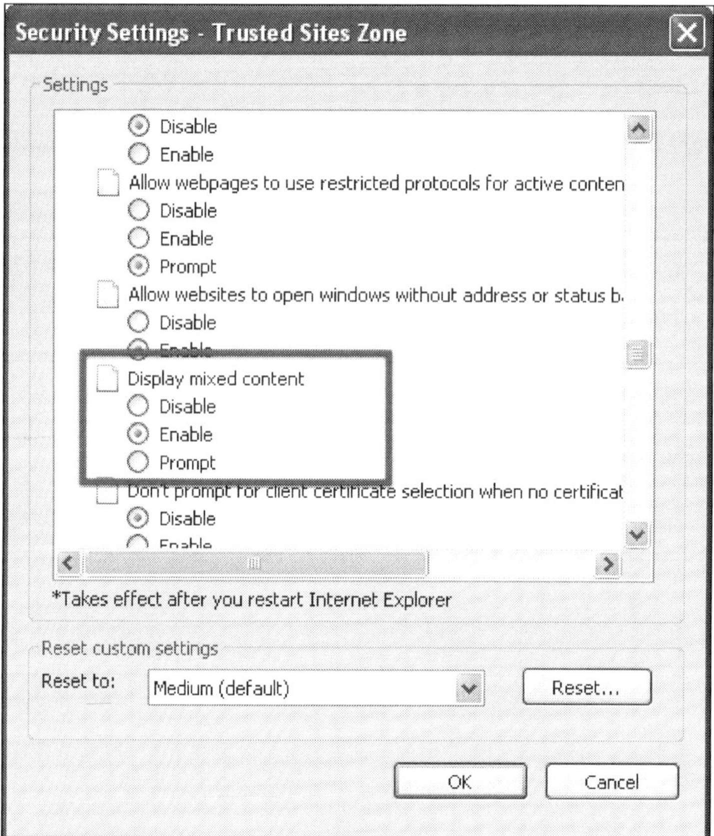

See also

▸ The *Embedding web videos* recipe in *Chapter 4, Working with Multimedia*

2
Personalizing Your Course

In this chapter, we will cover the following recipes:

- Using your profile to add personality
- Customizing navbar links
- Creating navigation groups
- Customizing your homepage with background images
- Using system variables to create customized content

Introduction

This chapter is all about customizing and personalizing your course. Using the powerful customization tools found in the Desire2Learn Learning Suite, we'll take the default course layout and transform it into a unique learning environment for your students. We'll start off by uploading a profile picture and completing your user profile, both of which are excellent first steps in adding some personality to the course. Next, we will edit the standard navigation bar, removing the tools you don't plan on using during the semester and adding some new links to the frequently used tools and external sites. We will take a look at the Learning Environment's newly redesigned theme editor and use it to apply a custom background image for our course. It's not all about design enhancements though; we'll wrap up by exploring a simple approach for displaying custom content to students.

Using your profile to add personality

Much like Facebook and other social networking sites, Desire2Learn Learning Suite users have access to a **Profile** page, where they can upload a user photo, identify hobbies and interests, and even provide links to other sites, such as Twitter or LinkedIn. Profile images are displayed throughout the system in various locations including the **Classlist** and **Discussions** tools. Completing your profile gives students a better idea of who you are and may help convince them to take a few minutes to complete their profiles as well.

Getting ready

Before accessing your course, you need to locate an image, in JPG format, to use as your profile picture. In addition, your role within the Learning Environment will need to have access to view and edit user profiles. Please be aware that each institution is able to customize the options to make them available in the profile tool; what you see in the screenshots that follow may be slightly different from what you see when following your own course.

How to do it...

In the following steps, we will edit our Desire2Learn Learning Suite profile. We'll use a free online web service to resize our profile picture before uploading it to the system.

1. Activate the personal context menu in the minibar and select the **Profile** option.

2. Fill in as much of the personal details as you'd like. If there's something you don't feel comfortable sharing (such as your birthday), then just leave that field blank.

3. Take a look at the example text under the social media URL fields. You can use the provided examples to create links to your Twitter, Facebook, and LinkedIn profile pages. Highlight the example text, copy it to your clipboard using the keyboard shortcut *Ctrl* + *C* (PC) or *Cmd* + *C*(Mac), and paste it in the text fields. Make sure you replace the placeholder text with your actual username:

Hometown:

Facebook:

e.g. http://www.facebook.com/myusername

4. Open a new tab in your web browser and navigate to www.picmonkey.com. Click and drag your profile picture over the browser window. Drop the image on the **Edit your photo** area.

5. Click on the **Resize edit** option. Make sure that the **Keep proportions** option is checked, then adjust the width (left text field) to **300** or less:

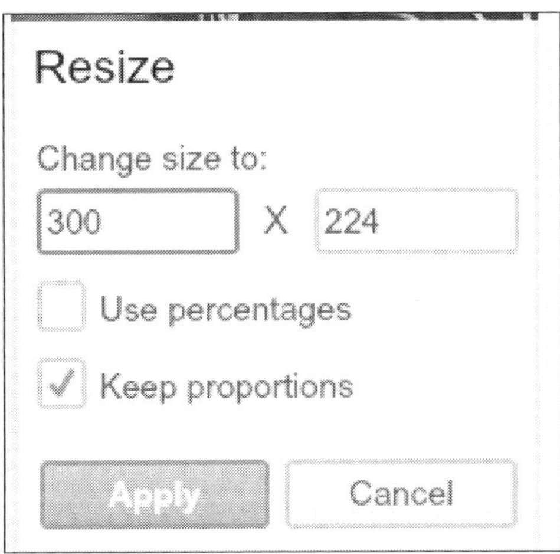

6. Click on the **Apply** button. Now, click on the **Save** button at the bottom of the window.

7. Finally, click on **Save Photo**, choose a name and location to save your resized image, and click on **Save**.

8. Return to your course and click on the **Change Picture** button.

9. Click on the **Choose File** button in the dialog box that appears.

10. Select the edited image we just saved. Then, click on **Open**.

11. Click on **Upload**.

How it works...

Almost any image you capture with a digital camera or mobile device is going to be much bigger than we should insert in a web page, so we use a web service, **PicMonkey**, to resize our image before uploading it to our course. There are plenty of other apps and services that are perfectly capable of resizing images, but I prefer PicMonkey because it is web-based and requires no registration or account setup. If you are more comfortable using a photo editor such as Photoshop or GIMP, please feel free to do so.

There's more...

You may be wondering why we chose 300 pixels for the width of our image in step 5. You've probably heard the term **megapixel** when reading product details for digital cameras. My mobile phone, for example, has an 8 megapixel sensor, which means that it can create images that are comprised of 8 million individual pixels (a megapixel is 1,000,000 pixels). The problem is that computer screens are typically only capable of showing a small fraction of that number of pixels. Although screen resolutions vary widely, 1024x768 is a fairly common resolution for a small desktop monitor – that's 1,024 pixels wide and 768 pixels in height. Multiply those numbers together and you'll discover the entire screen in our example is only showing 786,432 pixels. That's 1/8 of the pixels captured by the phone's sensor, and that's to fill the entire screen! We need to resize the image so that we aren't uploading files larger than they need to be.

While we can resize uploaded images in the Learning Environment's HTML editor, doing so only changes the size in which the image is displayed. Resizing in this manner does not affect the actual file size or resolution of the image itself. This may not be a big deal for students accessing the site from a high speed Internet connection, but those using dial-up or 3G broadband on their phones will appreciate the extra effort we're taking.

See also

- The *Customizing your homepage with delete background images* recipe

Customizing navbar links

In this recipe, we're going to customize our course navigation bar to make sure that students are able to access content and tools as easily as possible.

Getting ready

In order to complete this recipe, your role in the current course must have permissions to manage navbars.

How to do it...

We'll start by duplicating an existing navbar. Then, we'll remove any links to unused tools, and add links to other tools, and provide quick access to frequently used external websites.

1. Access your course and click on the **Manage Navigation &Themes** (small gear) icon that appears next to the course navigation bar.

2. Take note of the name of the navbar in the **Active Navbar** drop-down list. Let's copy the current navbar by locating it in the list and choosing the **Copy** option in the contextual menu

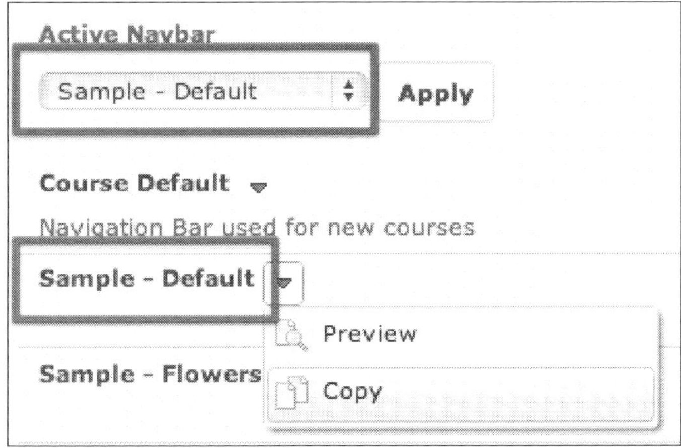

3. Once copied, access the new navbar by clicking on its title. Go ahead and provide a name and description for the navbar.

4. Remove unwanted links by hovering over each item in the **Links** area until an **X** icon appears in the top-right corner. Click on the **X** icon to remove the link (or group of links) from the navigation bar:

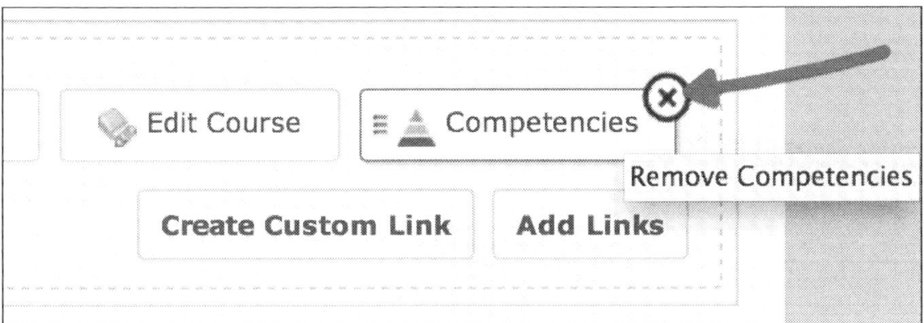

5. Click on the **Save** button once you've removed all the unwanted links.

6. Now let's add links to some frequently used system tools. Start by clicking on the **Add Links** button.

7. Select the checkboxes next to any tool you want to add to the navbar. You can click on any of the **Filter By:** links or enter a term in the **Search** bar to make finding the tools you want easier. Click on the **Add** button once you've selected the tools.

8. Now, let's add a custom, external link to your navbar by clicking on the **Create Custom Link** button.

9. Type a name for the link in the **Name** field.

10. Type a short description for the link in the **Description** text area.

11. Provide the address of an external site in the **URL** field.

12. Let's go ahead and click on the **Behavior** drop-down list and choose the **New window** option.

13. Change the width of the new window to **1024** pixels wide and **768** pixels high. While you're at it, go ahead and check both the options under **Browser Attributes**:

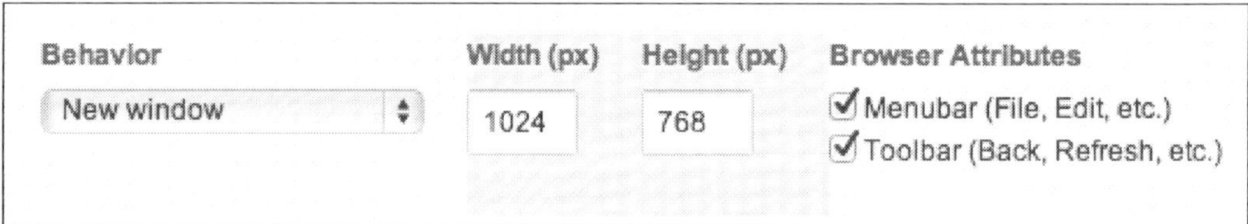

14. Click on the **Create** button when finished.

15. Click on the **Save and Close** button on the **Edit Navbar** page.

16. Let's finish by making our new navbar active in the current course. Simply select it from the **Active Navbar** drop-down list and click on the **Apply** button.

How it works...

We begin by creating a copy of the current navigation bar. Although we could have started a new one from scratch, modifying an existing navbar is usually easier when only minor changes are required. After providing a name and title, we streamlined our new navbar by removing links to any system tools that are not going to be used in the course. Next, we added links to any missing tools by clicking on the **Add Links** button and selecting items from the list of available tools. You can further customize the items in the menu bar by rearranging the order in which the links are displayed. To adjust the order, click-and-drag any item or group of items to a new location.

The **Create Custom Link** button is used to add links to external websites. The text you add to the **Name** field is what's displayed in your course navbar, so try to keep it as short as possible. You can optionally add an icon for each link by either dragging and dropping an icon into the browser or by using the **Add File** button. When directing students to content outside of the Learning Environment, I recommend opening links in a new window. In this recipe, we increased the size of the new browser window and checked the options to display standard browser controls in the new window. Feel free to experiment with different window sizes and options to find what works best for your course.

See also

> ▸ The *Creating navigation groups* and *Customizing your homepage with background images* recipes

Creating navigation groups

In past versions of the Learning Environment, giving students access to more tools typically meant adding more items to your course navigation bar. Version 10.0, however, adds the ability to create link groups, which helps simplify the user interface. By removing the distracting elements and organizing similar tools into groups, we will make it easier for students to find what they're looking for.

Getting ready

Since we're going to add custom groups of links to our course's navigation bar, your role in the course must have permissions to manage navbars. I'm also assuming that you already have an editable navbar to use in the following steps. If you don't yet have one, take a quick look at the previous recipe before moving forward.

How to do it...

In this recipe, we will create two groups of links for our course navbar—one containing links to external sites and another with links to the system tools.

1. Access your Desire2Learn Learning Suite course and click on the **Manage Navigation & Themes** (small gear) icon that appears next to the course's navigation bar.

2. Navigate to the **Custom Links** area of the tool

3. Click on the **Create Link Group** button. Then, provide a name and description for the new group.

4. Click on the **Create Link** button to create a new, custom link.

5. Enter a title and description for the link. Then, type the address of a website in the **URL** field:

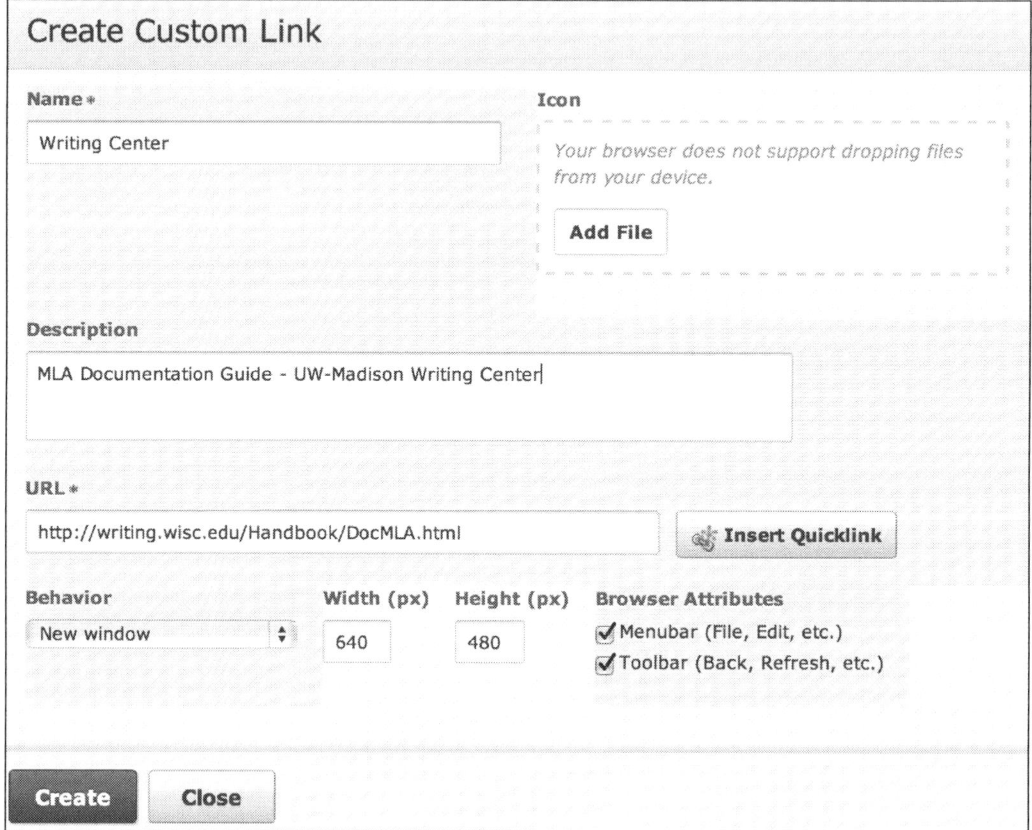

6. Since we are linking to an external site, let's choose the **New Window** option from the **Behavior** drop-down list.

7. Click on the **Create** button.

8. Repeat steps 5 to 9 to add a few more links to our new group. Click on the **Save** button when finished.

9. Let's add one more custom group to the navbar. However, this time we will create a group of system tools. Click on the **Create Link Group** button to get started.

10. Provide a title and description for the group. Then, click on the **Add Existing Link** button.

11. Select the checkboxes next to each of the links you'd like to add to the new group, and click on the **Add** button:

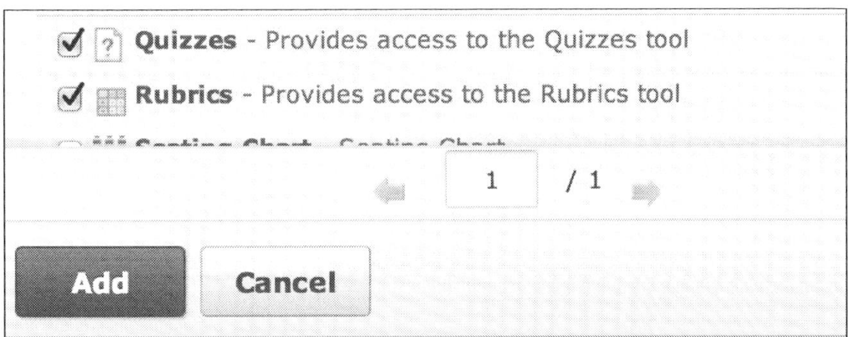

12. Click on the **Save** button.

13. Let's head back to the **Navbars** screen to add our new groups to the course's navbar.

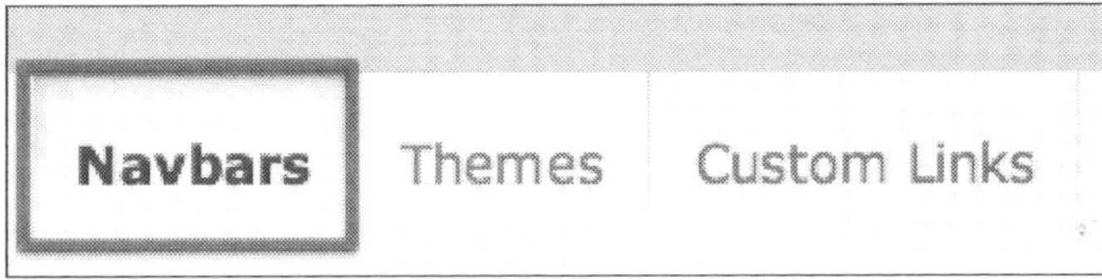

14. Click on the title of the navbar to which you want to add the new groups.

15. Click on the **Add Links** button in the **Links** area.

16. Click on **Custom Groups** to filter the list of available links. Then, check the boxes next to both of our new groups.

17. Click on the **Add** button.

18. Finally, click on the **Save and Close** button. You should now see your link groups in the course's navbar.

How it works...

Adding groups of links to your course means navigating between two different areas of the navbar editor—the **Navbars** and **Custom Links** tabs. You begin by visiting the **Custom Links** area to create and populate your groups with links. These can be either links to the built-in system tools or to external websites. After creating your groups, you can add them to a navbar by visiting the **Navbars** area.

As of version 10.0, there's no way to reorder links added to a custom link group. If you do need to change the order of links that you've already added to the group, then you'll need to delete them and create new ones.

Although we chose not to do so in this recipe, you can upload icons for both custom link groups and custom links that you create by dragging-and-dropping images into the **Icon** area or clicking by on the **Add File** button and selecting a file to upload. Be careful if you decide to add your own icons, as the system doesn't automatically resize the images you upload. If you do decide to create your own, I recommend saving them as 16x16 pixels PNG images with a transparent background. This is the format of the default system icons, and using the same settings with your images will help create a consistent user experience.

See also

> ▸ The *Customizing navbar links*, *Customizing your homepage with background images*, and *Using your profile to add personality* recipes

Customizing your homepage with background images

Themes allow you to alter the appearance of your course homepage and create a unique and inviting experience for your students. Using themes, you can adjust the margins, padding, and other visual characteristics of both the navbar and main content area. In this recipe, we'll focus on assigning custom background images to your course homepage using themes. After learning the basics, you can adjust the steps in this recipe to create your own custom look and feel.

Getting ready

We won't be discussing the actual creation of the custom artwork—I'm assuming that you've already created something using the image editor of your choice. You can use Photoshop, GIMP, or even online tools such as picmonkey.com in the creation process. You may even want to search Google or Flickr for Creative Commons licensed images if you aren't feeling too creative. In order to complete this recipe, your role in the course must have permissions to create themes. The following screenshot shows a sample of what we'll be creating:

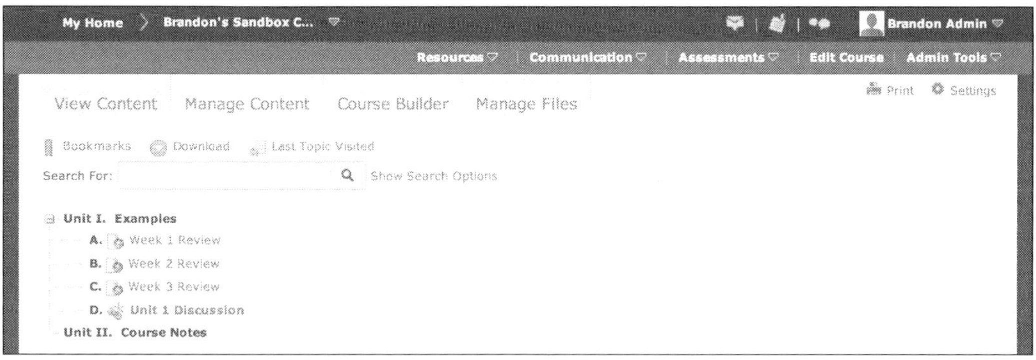

How to do it...

We're going to create a simple theme and apply it to an existing course. As you work through the recipe, think about how you can modify the steps to meet your own design goals.

1. Access your course and click on the **Manage Navigation & Themes** (small gear) icon that appears next to the course navigation bar.

2. Navigate to the **Themes** area of the tool. Then, click on the **Create Theme** button.

3. Provide a name and short description for the theme in the text fields provided.

4. Let's click on the **Change Layout** button and select the **Slim layout** option.

5. Click inside the **Navigation Background** area to load the **Navigation Background Properties** editor

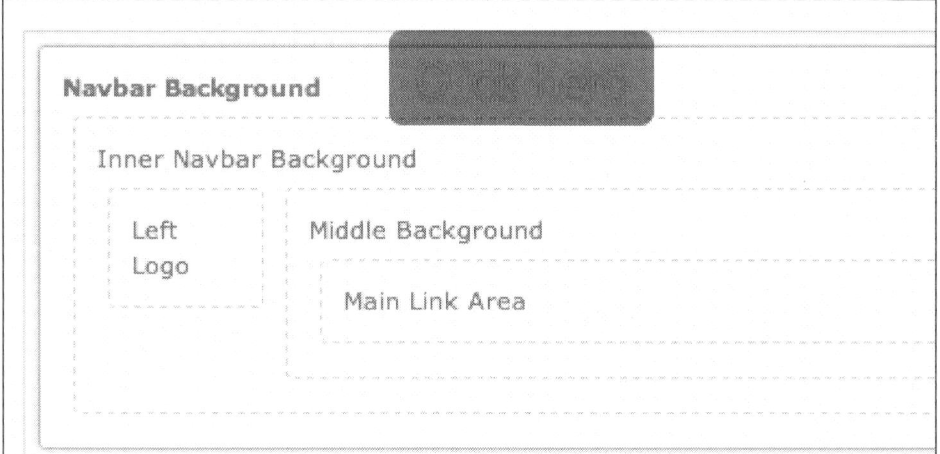

6. Let's change the background color of the navbar to dark blue by clicking on the paint bucket icon and clicking on the **More** button. Then, type `32699c` in the **Hex Value** textbox:

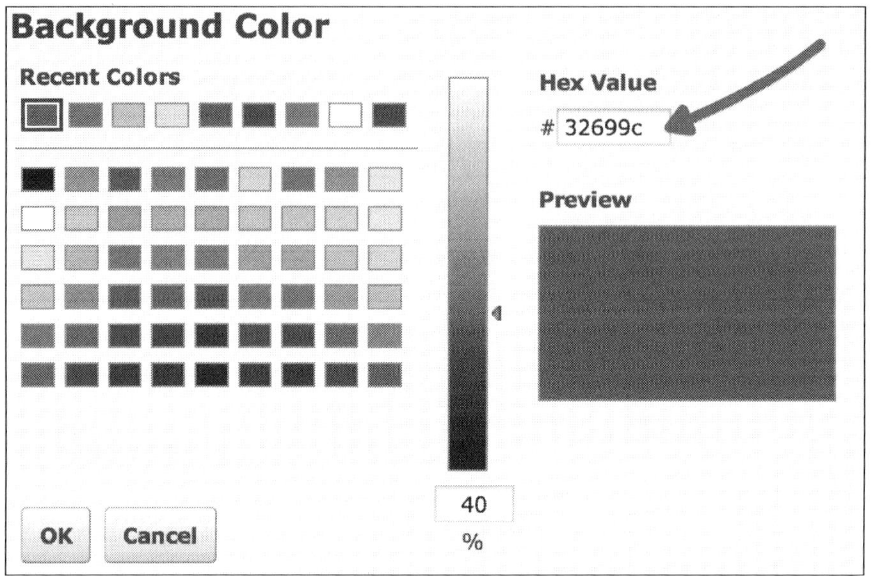

7. Before we move on, scroll down to the **Borders** section and assign a **Solid, Thin** line to the bottom border. In order to help separate it from the rest of the page, let's make the border slightly darker than the navbar background color. Using the preceding steps, assign a Hex value of **20588b**:

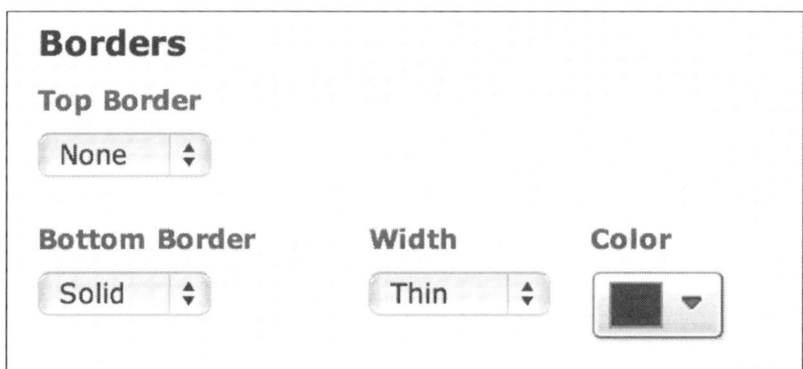

8. Now that we're done editing the navbar background properties, click on the **Hide Properties** button to dismiss the editor.

9. Click inside the **Main Links** area to edit its properties.

10. Choose the **Right Alignment** option in the **Link Alignment** drop-down list.

11. Choose the **Text Only** option in the **Display As** drop-down list.

12. Let's make the links a little more prominent by selecting the **Bold** option in the **Link Styles** section. In addition, change the color of the link text to white so that it stands out from the dark background:

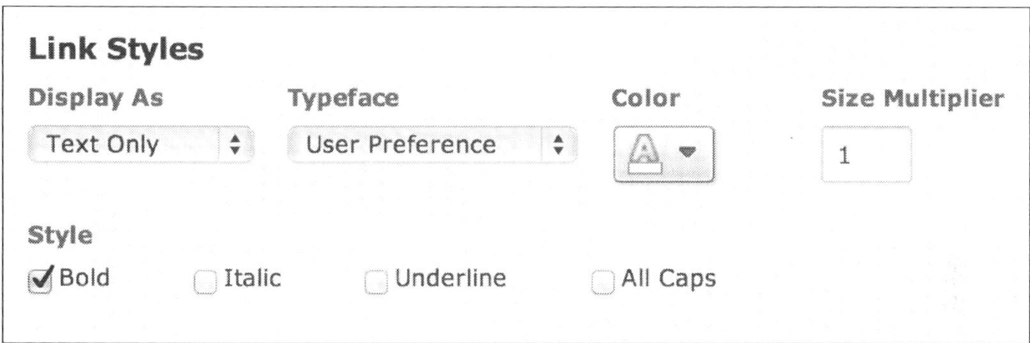

13. Click on the **Hide Properties** button.

14. I downloaded a dark gray repeating background image to use on both the left and right sides of the main content area. If you would like to follow along, you can download the image from `http://subtlepatterns.com/wild-oliva/`. Once downloaded, just unzip the folder and locate the `wild-oliva.png` file.

15. Click inside the **LeftPage Background** area.

16. Drag your background from your desktop and drop it on the **Background Image** target.

17. Select the **Repeat** option in the **Image Repeat** drop-down list:

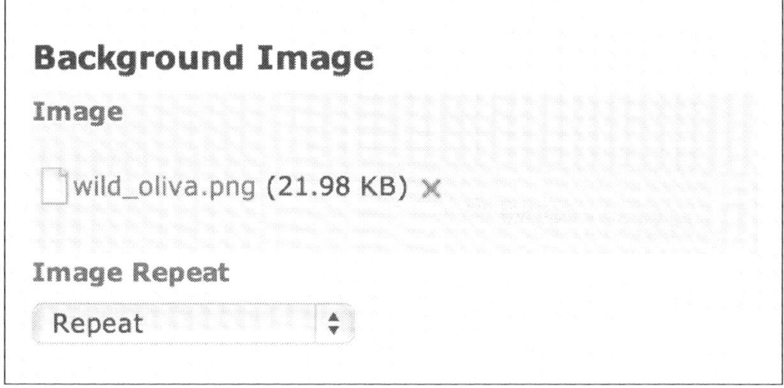

18. Click on the **Hide Properties** button.

19. Click on the **Right Page Background** area and repeat the preceding steps to assign the image as the background for the right side of the page. Remember to set the image as **Repeating**.

20. Click on the **Save and Close** button.

21. Let's navigate back to the **Navbars** area of the tool to activate a new navbar for the current course. Click on the **Navbars** link at the top of the page.

22. Click on the title of the current navbar. Then, click on the **Change Theme** button.

23. Select your new theme from the list of options and click on the **Update** button.

24. Click on the **Save and Close** button.

How it works...

You can create a new theme by either copying and then modifying an existing theme or by creating a new, blank theme from scratch, as we did in this tutorial. After creating and naming a theme, you assign a layout to determine how the navigation and logo elements are arranged on the page. If you make use of link groups in your course and don't need a lot of room for links in the navbar, then the **Simple** theme may work well for you. Otherwise, you may need to choose another layout, such as **Stacked**, which gives you more room for links.

You can easily modify the appearance of various elements by selecting the element on the **Edit Theme** page and adjusting properties such as the background image, background color, border thickness and color, and more. When selecting colors, choose between the pre-defined color swatches or click on the **More** link for more options. You can even provide a Hex value if you're trying to use specific colors, such as those specified in your school's style guide, in your homepage design. In this recipe, we visited the **Navbar Background** and **Main Link** areas, but you can create more complicated designs by exploring some of the other areas as well. The minibar, however, is only editable at the institutional level, so you won't be able to modify it for your own course.

You can assign background images and colors to the whole page, the left panel, and the right panel by selecting each section on the **Edit Theme** page and modifying each element's properties. Since each of these areas can have a separate background color and image, it's possible to create some much more complex designs that what we've done here. We created a simple, minimal interface by assigning a repeating texture to the background of both the left and right panels. Although you can use larger non-repeating images, if you'd like, just be aware that larger images may increase the time it takes to load pages in your course, especially if your students don't have access to a high-speed Internet connection. Keep an eye on the **Theme Preview** area as you work to get an idea how your current design will look in a real course.

- The *Using your profile to add personality* recipe
- The *Finding Creative Commons licensed images* recipe in *Chapter 4, Working with Multimedia*

Using system variables to create customized content

The title for this recipe may sound scary if you're not a programmer, but have no fear; system variables are actually very easy to use and can be a great tool for customizing your course's content! System variables, or replace strings, are placeholders that that can be inserted in the course e-mail, content, widgets, news items, or just about anywhere you have access to the HTML editor. The values of these variables are dynamically set when a user accesses a page containing them. If you've used mail merge in a word-processing application, then you're already familiar with this concept.

Getting ready

We don't need anything special to complete this recipe—just a Desire2Learn Learning Suite course and access to the news tool would suffice.

How to do it...

In this recipe, we will walk through the process of creating a news item, welcoming each student to your course. Although we only create the item once, each student that views the page will see a custom message with their own names.

1. Access your course and click on the **New News Item** icon in the news widget.

2. Type a message in the headline text field. Provide a subject for the news item in the Headline text field. If you want to mention the name of the course, replace the actual name with {OrgUnitName}.

3. In the content area, type:

   ```
   Hi {FirstName},
   Thanks for taking {OrgUnitName}. I look forward to having you in
   class this semester.
   ```

4. Click on the **Publish** button when finished.

5. Now, head back to the course's **Home** page and take a look at the news item we just created. You should see your first and last names in the headline along with the name of the course and your first name in the body of the news item:

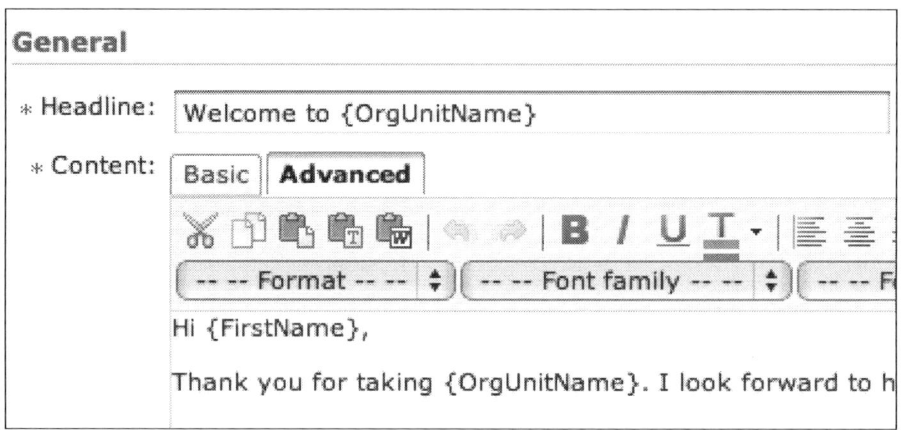

How it works...

When a page is requested from the server, system variables such as `{FirstName}`, `{LastName}`, and `{OrgUnitId}`, are replaced with information from the current user's account and the current course offering information. If John Doe views this particular news item in **Accounting Course**, he would see a message welcoming him to accounting. Other variables are also available, but these three are probably the most useful for most instructors. Try searching the Web for the phrase `Desire2Learn replace strings` if you're curious about other options.

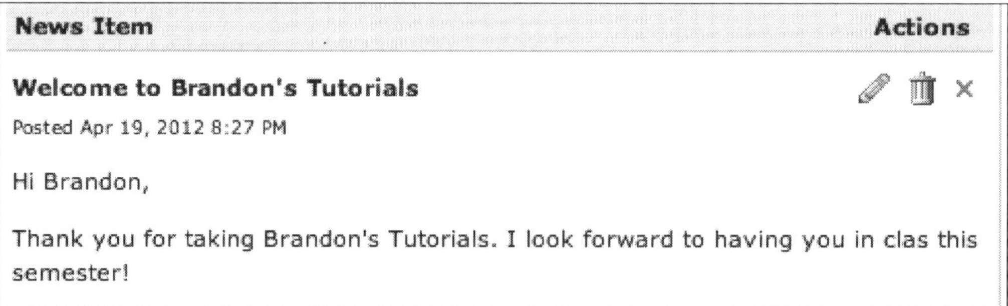

3
Getting Materials into Your Course

In this chapter, we will cover:

- Outlining a new course using Course Builder
- Reorganizing an existing course with Course Builder
- Getting existing Microsoft Word documents into your course
- Working with PowerPoint presentations
- Updating course files without deleting the original topics
- Uploading folders to batch create course content
- Adding content from the Learning Object Repository
- Using Google Docs to allow multiple download formats

Introduction

This chapter discusses several tools and techniques for getting material into your Desire2Learn Learning Environment course. If you've spent time developing or modifying a course, there's a good chance you're already familiar with the standard creation tools found in the **Content** area, so we aren't going to spend time reviewing them here. Instead, the recipes in this chapter focus on using lesser-known system tools and third-party applications that will increase your productivity and help you create materials that can be easily accessed by students.

We start off by using the **Course Builder** tool to quickly layout the structure of a new course. Course Builder, despite its name, is also the perfect tool for rearranging or restructuring an existing course, so we will take a look at how you can do that in the second recipe.

Many instructors like to share Microsoft Word and PowerPoint files with students. However, these file formats can be problematic in an online course because not all students have access to the software required to view them. The next few recipes explore ways of converting these documents to more accessible formats, such as PDF.

Although we typically work with course materials in the Content tool, the Learning Environment's File Manager tool gives us access to some great timesaving features. We'll use it to update files attached to content topics (without needing to delete and recreate the topic). We will also use the tool to upload a `.zip` file containing multiple documents, and create topics linked to those files.

The **Learning Object Repository (LOR)** is a centralized location where you can both share and retrieve content. We can use dynamic linking of LOR resources to make it easier to keep our content up-to-date. By linking to the most recent version of an object, you don't have to worry about editing the same object in multiple courses when a change is necessary.

We'll wrap up the chapter with a recipe that uses Google Docs to present information and facilitate collaboration between students. Google Docs offers some real advantages over posting regular MS Office files, such as the ability to edit online, download in multiple formats, and chat with other viewers of the document.

Outlining a new course using Course Builder

In this recipe, we'll use the Course Builder tool to quickly outline the structure of a new course. Almost everything we'll walk through in this recipe could be accomplished using other tools within the system; however, Course Builder saves us time by presenting everything we need in one place. In addition, the tool's intuitive drag-and-drop interface makes organizing and rearranging materials a breeze. We will learn how to use Course Builder's `copy` function to duplicate the structure of your course's content, so that we don't have to spend our time performing repetitive tasks.

The example we're using here is very simple. After learning the basics in this recipe, you should be able to apply the same techniques in your own courses, which probably have a much more complex structure.

Getting ready

We are going to focus on creating the structure of a course in this section, so you don't need anything to follow along besides access to the Course Builder tool. When you apply these techniques to your own course, it's a good idea to have a basic outline of your course available, along with the actual content you'll be adding to the course.

How to do it...

In the following steps, we will use placeholder objects to create a simple module for a course. Then, we will duplicate the module to illustrate how Course Builder can help quickly layout a complete course structure.

1. Access your course and navigate to the **Content** tool.

2. Click on the **Course Builder** tab.

3. Click and drag a **Module** placeholder icon from the **Build Outline** section of the toolbox area to the canvas:

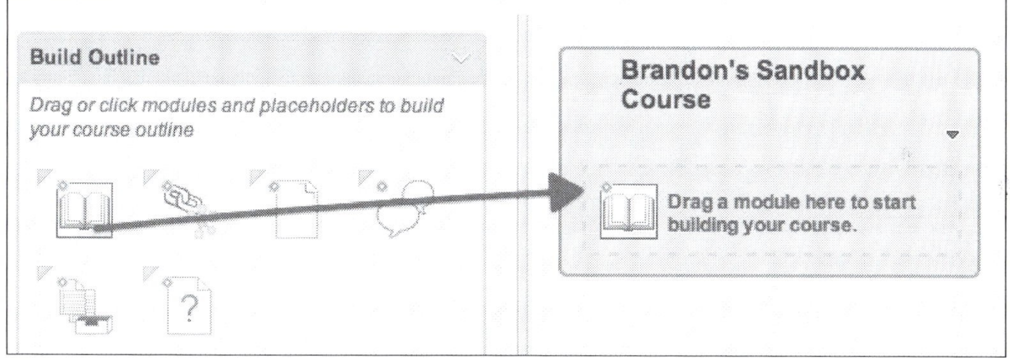

4. Provide a name for the module. I am going to call mine `Introduction`. Click on **Create**.

5. Drag a **File** placeholder from the **Build Outline** section and drop it on the module we just created.

6. Change the name to **Reading**. Then click on the **Create button**.

7. Drag a **Discussion** placeholder and drop it in the **Introduction** moc

8. Let's keep the default name and click on the **Create** button.

9. Drag a **Quiz** placeholder and drop it in the **Introduction** module. We can keep the default name for this one as well. Click on **Create** when prompted. Your module should now look similar to the following screenshot:

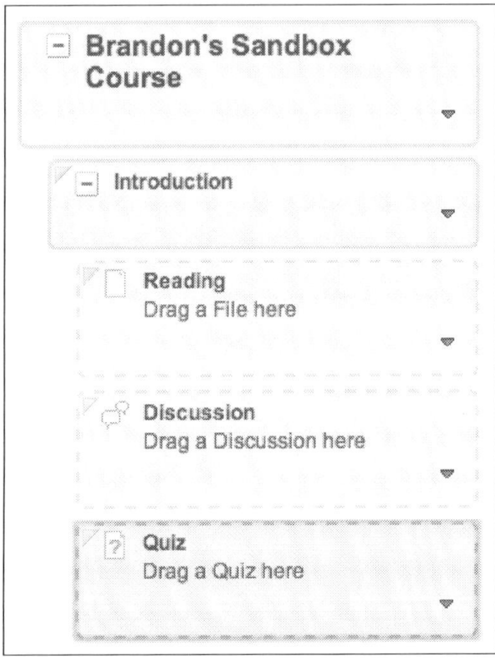

10. Click on the drop-down context menu for the **Introduction** module. Choose **Copy Structure** from the list of available actions:

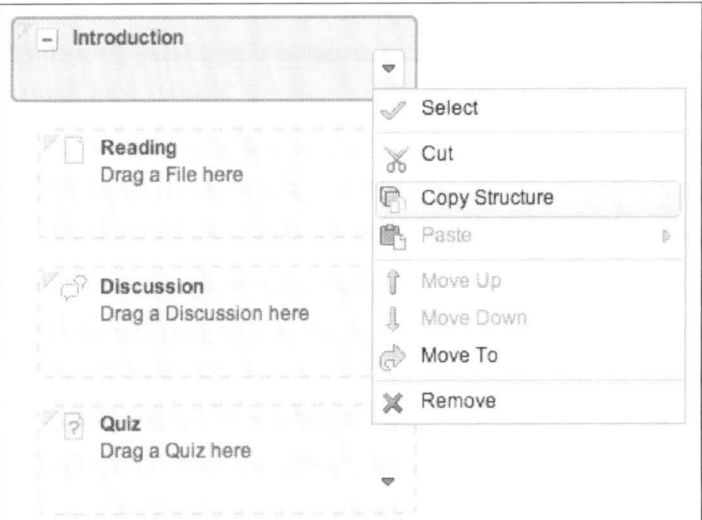

11. Click on the context menu for the top node on the canvas. This time, select **Paste** from the list of actions.

12. Repeat the process two more times, so that you have a total of four identical modules.

13. Click on the second **Introduction** module to select it. The information in the **Selected Node** panel (right column) will change to display the properties of the currently-selected item. Click on the **Edit Module** link.

14. Change the title and click on **Save**. I named mine `Module I`, but feel free to name yours to whatever you'd like.

15. Repeat the same process for the last two **Introduction** modules.

How it works...

We start off this recipe by navigating to the **Course Builder** tab in the **Content** tool, but you can also find a link to **Course Builder** on the **Edit Course** page. Next, we create a module placeholder by dragging a **Module** item from the **Build Outline** section of the **Toolbox** widget to the canvas. We then complete the structure of the module by dragging and dropping other objects into it. In our example, this includes file, discussion, and quiz placeholders.

Objects in the **Build Outline** section are placeholders that you can use when you want to layout a course but aren't quite ready to actually create the objects in your course. For example, we've included a reading assignment, discussion topic, and quiz in our example module. However, these items aren't available in the course until we replace the placeholders with actual objects. We'll take a look at how to create those objects in just a minute.

Once we define the basic structure of our prototype module, we use Course Builder's **Copy Structure** function to duplicate the module for each unit in our example course. Then, we select each new module and change its name in the **Selected Node** panel. The information displayed in that panel will change based on the item selected in the canvas.

There's more...

So far, we've barely scratched the surface of what's possible in Course Builder. You probably noticed the **Add Content** and **Browse Tools** sections of the toolbox. Let's take a quick look at how you'd use those tools when developing a course.

Creating objects

The objects we added to the canvas earlier in this tutorial are just placeholder items. If you access the course's other tools, you'll notice that while we added discussion topics, quizzes, and content items in Course Builder, they do not appear anywhere else in the course. Placeholders are great for creating an outline or defining the structure of a course. At some point, however, you're going to want to replace those placeholders with actual items that can be accessed by students. We'll use the **Create Objects** section to do that.

Click on the small **+** symbol on the left side of the **Introduction** module to expand it. Then drag a **Discussion** item from **Add Content** over the canvas and drop it on the existing placeholder. When you release the object, you will be presented with a **New Discussion** dialog box. Simply fill in the required fields, and click on **Create**. Notice that rather than the dashed outline of a placeholder object, the item now has a solid outline indicating that the object now exists in the course:

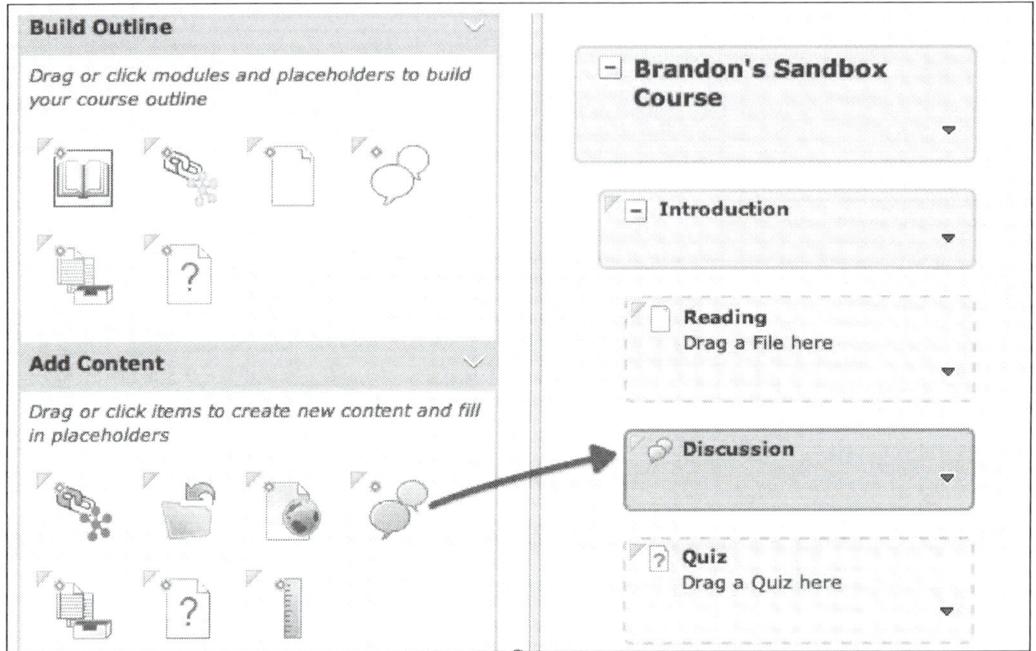

Go ahead and take a look in **Course Content**. You should now see a quick link that links to a discussion topic. If you navigate to the discussion tool, you will see that the topic has been added there as well.

In our example, we chose to start with placeholders and created actual objects later, by dragging items over from the **Create Objects** section of the toolbox. You don't necessarily have to follow the same process in your course. If you're ready to create actual objects right away, simply skip the placeholder step and drag items from the **Add Content** panel from the beginning.

Browsing objects

So far, we've created new placeholders and objects by dragging items from the appropriate sections of the **Toolbox** pane. What if we want to include other objects in our outline items, such as discussion topics and course files, already in our course? You can do that using the **Browse Tools** section of the toolbox.

Start by clicking on the type of content you're interested in adding to the canvas. Once you've found an item, drag it from the left column over to the canvas and release it. A quicklink to that item is now accessible from your **Content** tool.

See also

▸   The *Reorganizing an existing course with Course Builder* recipe

Reorganizing an existing course with Course Builder

If you've ever tried making major revisions to the structure of an existing course, you're probably aware that rearranging the display order of content and moving topics from one module to another requires quite a few mouse clicks. Moving one or two items into a new module isn't too bad, but rearranging an entire course can be quite cumbersome. Luckily, we can use the Course Builder tool to dramatically speed up the process. In this recipe, we'll use the tool's drag-and-drop interface to both reorder topics and move items from one module to another.

Getting ready

You're going to need some content in Course Builder to work with. If you'd like to follow along with me, access the Course Builder tool and create a structure matching the following screenshot:

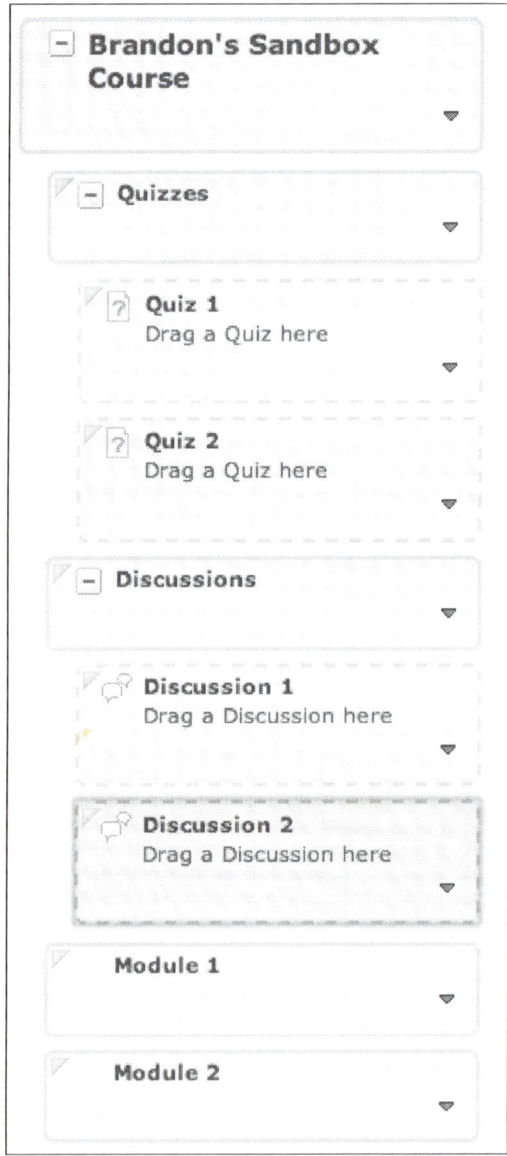

Take a look at the previous recipe if you need help getting started. Or, feel free to adapt the steps listed in the following section to match your own course.

1. Access your course and navigate to the **Content** tool.

2. Click the **Course Builder** tab.

3. Expand the **Quizzes** module (if it isn't already) by clicking on the **+** symbol to the left of the module name.

4. Click and drag **Quiz 1** from its current location to the **Module 1** node. The background color for the module will turn orange, indicating that it is selected. Once the background color changes, drop the quiz in the module.

5. Let's go ahead and move **Quiz 2** to **Module 2** using the same technique described in the previous steps.

6. Since we no longer need the **Quizzes** module, we can delete it by choosing the **Remove** option from the module's context menu:

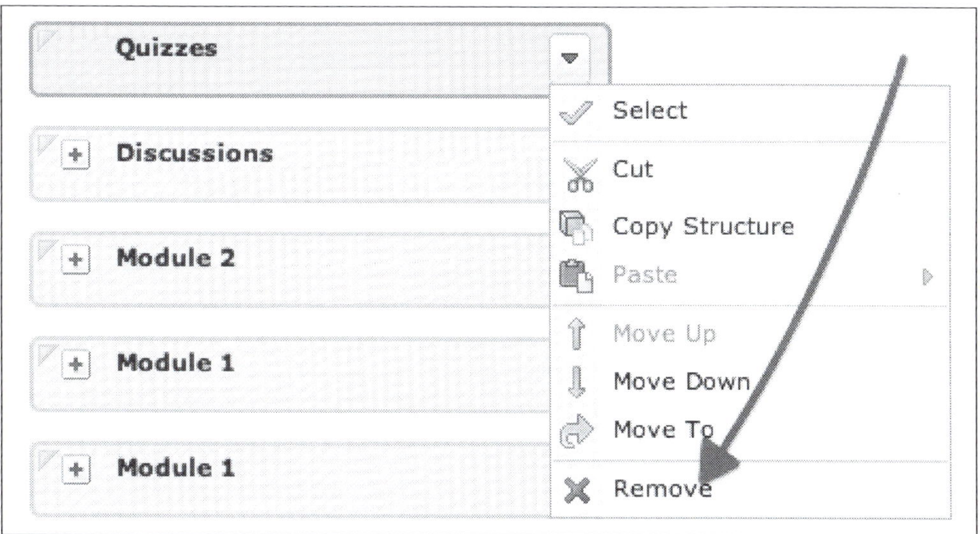

7. Let's drag and drop **Discussion 1** into the correct module. Instead of dropping it on the **Module 1** node, hover just above the **Quiz 1** item until you see a thin, black line, as shown in the following screenshot. You can release the mouse button when the line is in the correct location:

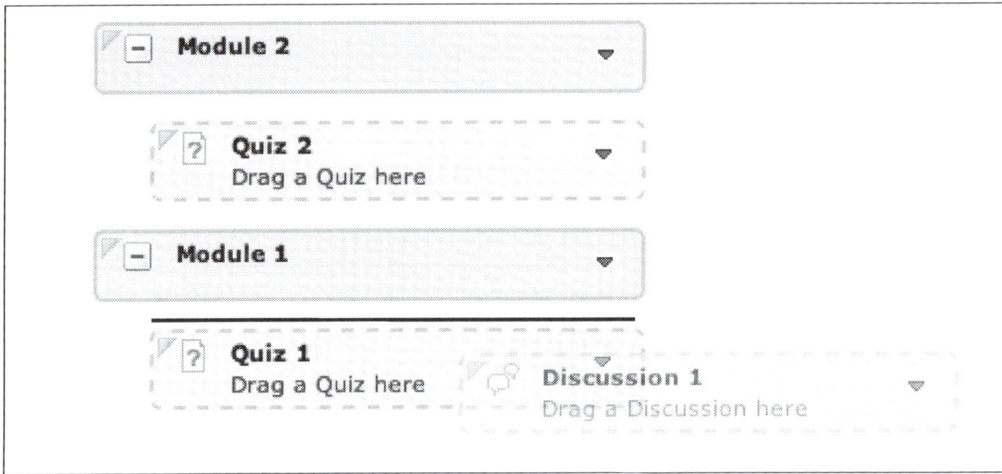

8. Go ahead and move **Discussion 2** into **Module 2**, as described in the previous steps. Then, delete the **Discussions** module.

9. It doesn't make a lot of sense to have **Module 2** before **Module 1**, so let's drag **Module 2** below **Module 1**.

How it works...

In this recipe, we explored two ways of restructuring content using Course Builder—moving items from one module to another and rearranging the order of items on the canvas. If we had used the standard Content tools, we would have needed to use two separate tools, one to move the topics between modules and the other to reorder our content. However, Course Builder allows us to complete both of these actions quite easily using an intuitive drag-and-drop interface.

See also

▸ The *Outlining a new course using Course Builder* recipe

Getting the existing Microsoft Word documents into your course

You probably have materials created in Microsoft Word that you'd like to be able to share with your students. Uploading `.doc` or `.docx` files to the content area of your course is a simple task of using the Learning Environment's built-in tools. However, students need to have MS Office (or at least the Word Viewer application) installed on their PCs in order to view the documents. This recipe shows how to create an HTML file from a Word document using D2L's standard HTML editor.

Getting ready

You'll need a copy of Microsoft Word installed on your computer to complete this recipe. The screenshots in the following sections are from Microsoft Office 2011 for Mac, but you should be able to follow along with any recent version of the program for either the Mac or Windows operating systems.

How to do it...

We are going to create a new Word document and convert it into an accessible HTML file in our course. The key point here is to use the structure elements in the **Styles** ribbon (Heading 1, Heading 2, and so on) to format our text.

1. Open MS Word and create a new, blank document.

2. Let's start by creating a heading for the document. Type `About This Class` and press the _Return_ key.

3. Compose a paragraph or two describing the class to your students. Don't apply any formatting yet—we'll take care of that in a few minutes. Press the _Return_ key again when you're finished.

4. Let's add one more section to our sample document. Type `About the Book` and press the _Return_ key again.

5. Enter some basic information about the course textbook.

6. Highlight the first heading, and click on the **Heading 1** button in the **Styles** section of the **Home** ribbon:

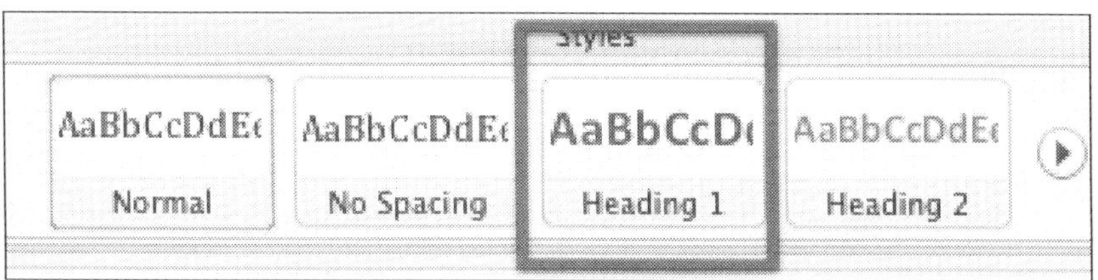

7. Highlight the second heading, **About the Book**, and click on the **Heading 2** button.

8. Select all of the text in the document using the keyboard shortcut *Ctrl + A* (PC) or *Cmd + A* (Mac). Then, copy the text to the clipboard by pressing *Ctrl + C* (PC) or *Cmd + C* (Mac).

9. Access the content area of your course. Click on the **Add Content** button and choose the **New File** option.

10. Choose a module for the topic, provide a title, and position your cursor inside the content `WYSIWYG` editor.

11. Access the **Advanced** toolbar, and click on the **Paste from Word** icon:

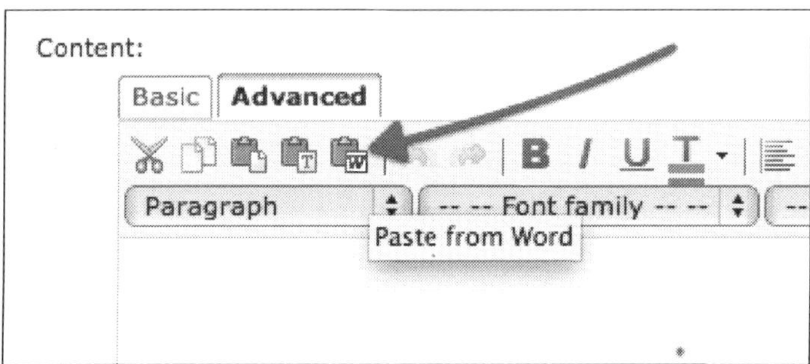

12. Press *Ctrl + V* (PC) or *Cmd + V* (Mac) to paste the selected text into the **Paste From Word** pop-up window.

13. Click on the **Insert** button.

14. Click on the **Save and Close** button once the pop-up window closes.

How it works...

When working in MS Word, it's important to apply text formatting using buttons from the **Styles** ribbon. Formatting applied in this fashion will work well when text is pasted into D2L's HTML editor. Using these pre-defined styles also helps create a structured, meaningful webpage that is more accessible to students using screen readers. On the other hand, applying formatting by manually choosing the font, color, or weight of the text from the **Font** section of the ribbon can add unnecessary code to your HTML document. Formatting applied in this manner is also meaningless to students with screen readers.

Suppose, for example, you're creating a study guide for you course and want to emphasize key paragraphs in the document. You could change the look of the text by selecting options from the **Font** section of the toolbar:

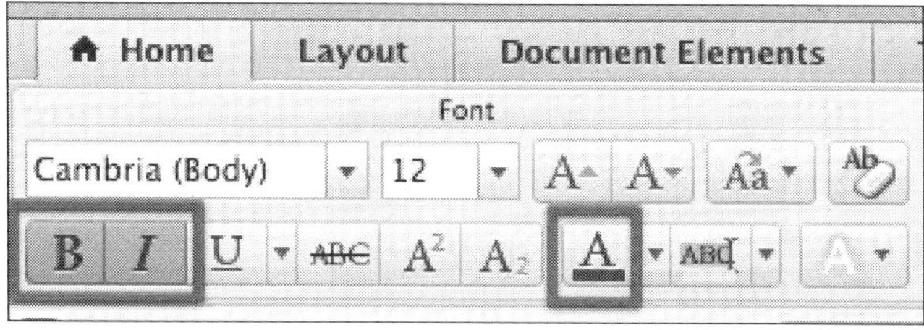

After pasting the text into the Learning Environment's content editor, you could view the HTML source and see something similar to the following screenshot:

```
</head>
<body style="font-family: 'PTSansRegular', Verdana, sans-serif;">
<p><b><i>Lorem ipsum dolor sit amet, consectetur adipiscing elit. Fusce
nec, vehicula quis sapien. Mauris id erat nisl, in consequat sem. Maecen
Maecenas vel felis eget risus vulputate ullamcorper. Curabitur erat dui,
congue. Pellentesque mattis euismod lectus, et venenatis metus egestas e
</body>
</html>
```

Notice that the styles referenced here don't tell us anything about the content itself. In addition, each time you want to apply the same style to a new paragraph, you would have to remember the initial combination of settings and choose them again. Changing the formatting of this text at a later date would introduce additional problems. You would need to revisit each block of text and make your changes to the text style manually.

Let's take a look at another example. This time, I've created a new style for the text using MS Word's **Style** ribbon. Each time I want to assign this style to a block of text, I just select the text and choose the appropriate style from the ribbon. When copied and pasted into the content editor, the code is much more meaningful, as you can see in the following screenshot. Instead of meaningless inline styles, this time our paragraph has been assigned a CSS class, which we can define once and easily use multiple times throughout our document or course. Take a look at the *Using CSS to style content* recipe for additional information on using CSS in your course.

```
<p class="ImportantInformation">Lorem ipsum dolor sit a
malesuada id sagittis nec, vehicula quis sapien. Mauris
quis, ornare et odio. Maecenas vel felis eget risus vul
nec tortor rhoncus congue. Pellentesque mattis euismod
```

It's also important to use the **Paste From Word** icon when copying and pasting text from MS Word. Pasting directly into the content editor can result in extraneous formatting that can cause problems later on. Although recent versions of the content editor are better at removing this formatting, it's still a good idea to use the **Paste From Word** icon.

Our example document doesn't include any images. Unfortunately, images cannot be copied and pasted form Word to the Desire2Learn Learning Environment. Instead, you should save each image as a file on your computer and use the content editor's **Insert Image** icon to upload each file separately.

There's more...

So far, we've discussed converting Word documents to HTML format. Since students will be accessing your site through a web browser, converting to a web format is typically the best option. However, if the document implements special layouts (such as text columns) or is intended to be printed by students, saving as a PDF may be a better alternative. PDFs can be uploaded to your course as attachments in many of the system's tools (including **news items** and **dropbox folders)** or uploaded into the **Content** area by choosing the **Upload File** option when creating a new topic.

Creating a PDF

MS Word 2007 and onwards offers a handy PDF option under the **Save** menu. To save a document as a PDF, simply choose **File | Save As**, and then select the **PDF** option.

If you're using a version of Word that doesn't support saving documents in the PDF format, take a look at **CutePDF Writer**. When installed, this free piece of software adds a virtual printer to your computer. PDFs can be then be easily created by sending your Word document, or any other file, to the CutePDF printer. You can find out more about CutePDF Writer at the following URL: `http://www.cutepdf.com/Products/CutePDF/writer.asp`. CutePDF isn't the only PDF creation utility out there. The web-based tool **Zamzar** (`http://www.zamzar.com`) allows you to convert between many file formats including PDF.

See also

- The *Working with PowerPoint presentations* and *Using Google Docs to allow multiple download formats* recipes
- *Using CSS to style content* in *Chapter 5, Diving into HTML Code*

Working with PowerPoint presentations

Many instructors use PowerPoint presentations in their traditional and online classes. In order to view these presentations, however, students need to have either MS Office or PowerPoint viewer installed on their computers. In addition, students sometimes experience compatibility issues between different versions (and operating systems) even when they do have the software installed. In this recipe, we will learn to save PowerPoint presentations in the more accessible PDF format. Although this format is not without its own shortcomings, you'll lose transitions and animations; the software needed to view PDFs is a free download and may already be installed on most computers.

Getting ready

You'll need a copy of Microsoft PowerPoint installed on your computer to complete this recipe. The following screenshots are from Microsoft Office 2010 for Windows, but you should be able to follow along with any recent version of the program for either the Mac or Windows operating systems.

How to do it...

In addition to converting a PowerPoint presentation to a PDF, we're going to publish using the handout format, which allows us to fit multiple slides per page. I recommend this option if students will be printing the file.

1. Open an existing PowerPoint presentation.
2. Click on **File**, and then choose the **Save As** option.
3. Choose **PDF** in the **Save as type:** drop-down list.
4. Click on the **Options** button.

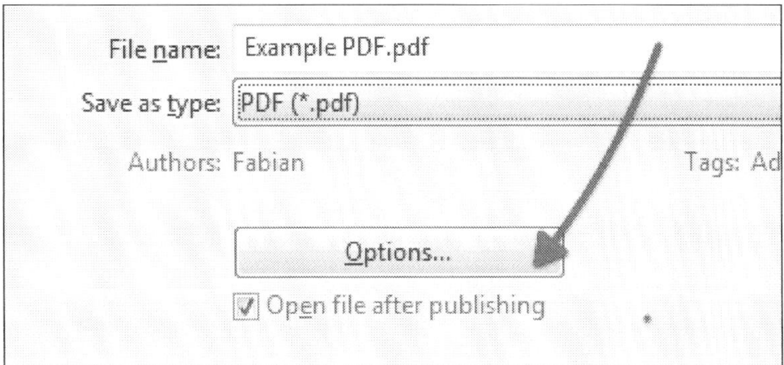

5. In the **Publish what:** field, choose the **Handouts** option:

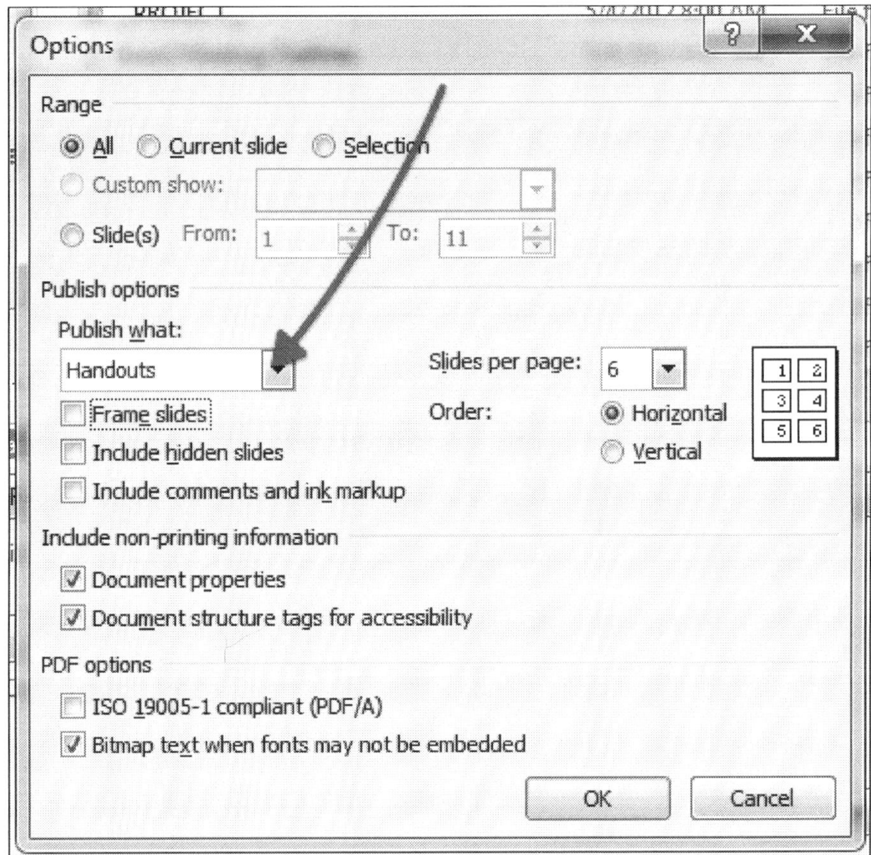

6. Let's change the desired number of slides per page to **6** in the drop-down menu to the right.

7. Click on the **OK** button.

How it works...

In order to save paper and make printing easier for students, we've chosen to publish a handout with multiple slides per page. We chose six slides per page in the preceding example, but you can certainly decrease that amount if your slides include detailed illustrations or contain large amounts of text information.

There's more...

The preceding example should work well for Windows users who have the most recent versions of Microsoft Office. Mac users and individuals with older versions of the Office Suite for Windows can still create PDF handouts using different procedures.

Creating PDF handouts on the Mac operating system

Mac users aren't given the option to publish handouts in the **Save As** menu of Office 2011. However, we can use the OS's built-in PDF functionality in the **Print** menu.

1. Access the **File** menu and choose the **Print** option.

2. Choose **Handouts (6 slides per page)** from the **Print What:** drop-down list:

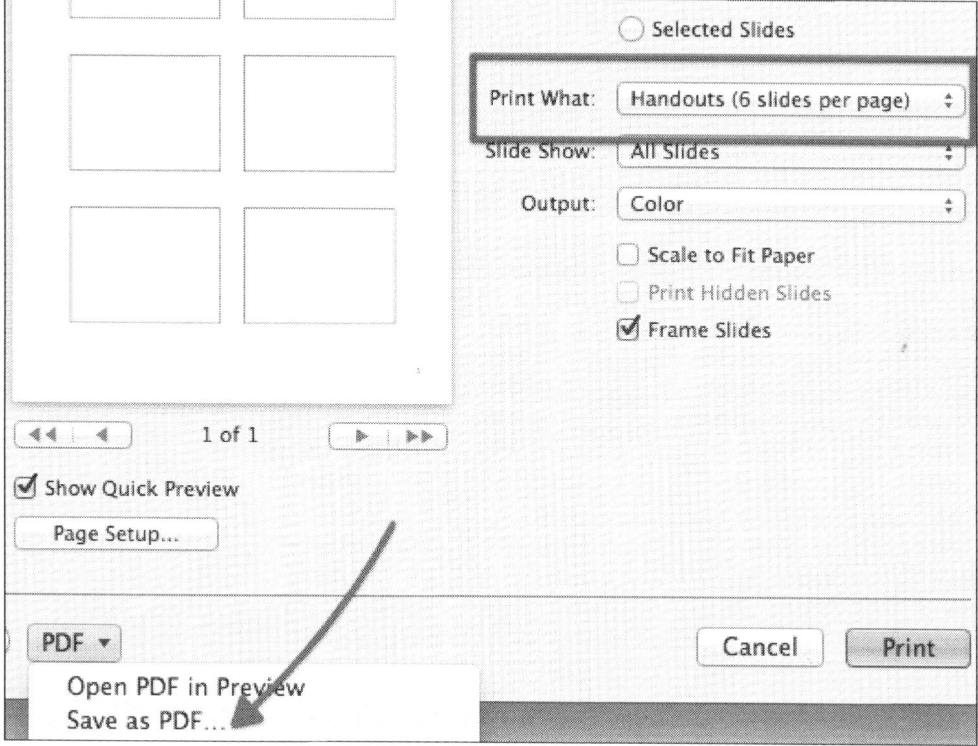

3. Click on the PDF button in the bottom left corner of the window, and then choose the **Save as PDF** option.

4. Enter a name for the file and click on the **Save** button.

Creating PDF handouts using CutePDF Writer

Unfortunately, you'll need to download a third-party tool for creating PDFs if you're using Office 2003. A Google search reveals plenty of options for commercial PDF creation software, including Adobe's own Acrobat and Acrobat Pro titles. For most users, however, a free utility called CutePDF Writer will work just fine.

You can download the application from the following URL: `http://www.cutepdf.com/Products/CutePDF/writer.asp`. Once downloaded and installed, a new printer named CutePDF will appear on your list of available printers. To create a PDF handout, access the **Print** menu, choose handouts, and select the new printer. You'll then be prompted for a location to save the file.

See also

> ▶ The *Using Google Docs to allow multiple download formats* in *Chapter 3, Getting Course Materials into D2L*

Updating course files without deleting the original topics

The Desire2Learn Learning Environment gives us an easy way to upload files created outside the system, such as PDFs and images, and link to them from a course's content area. Unlike documents created using the system's HTML editor, there's not an easy way to edit or update these files. In fact, many instructors simply delete the topic all together and re-upload another copy when a change is needed. In this recipe, we'll use the File Manager tool to quickly upload updated versions of existing files. We'll start out by creating a topic linking to a peer evaluation form saved as a PDF. We will then change the document and upload our new version to the course.

Getting ready

In order to complete this recipe, you'll need a document to upload to your course. I'm going to be using a PDF in the following example, but feel free to use whatever type of document you'd like.

How to do it...

We will start out by creating a new topic and uploading a file through the Content tool. Then, we will replace the document by uploading a new document with the same file name in the Manage Files tool.

1. Access your course and navigate to the **Content** tool.

2. Click on the **Add Content** button and choose the **Upload File** option.

3. Choose a module for the topic, provide a title and use the **Choose File** button to upload the PDF document from your desktop.

4. Click on the **Save and Close** button when finished.

5. Now, take a few minutes to modify the file you just added to your course. Proceed to the next step when you're ready to upload the new version.

6. Click on the **Manage Files** tab at the top of the **Manage Content** page.

7. Use the folder tree in the left column to select the directory of the file we previously uploaded. Once selected, use the **Upload** icon in the header of the right column to upload an updated version of the file. Click on the icon, and then choose a file from your desktop:

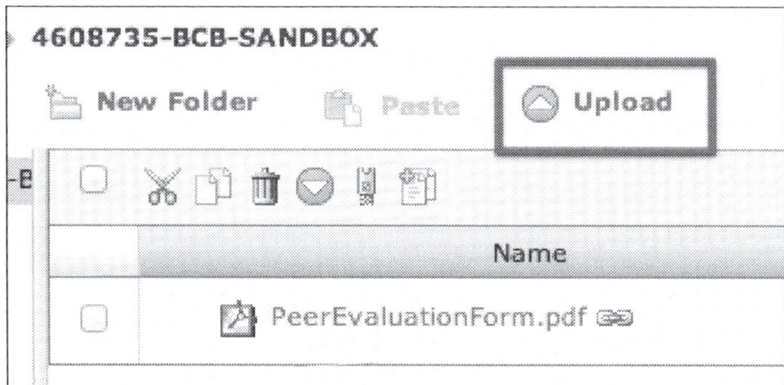

8. Choose the same file we just uploaded through the **Content** tool. Click on the **Upload** button.

9. When presented with the **Confirm File Replace** dialog box, check the box next to the original version of the document, and click on the **Overwrite** button:

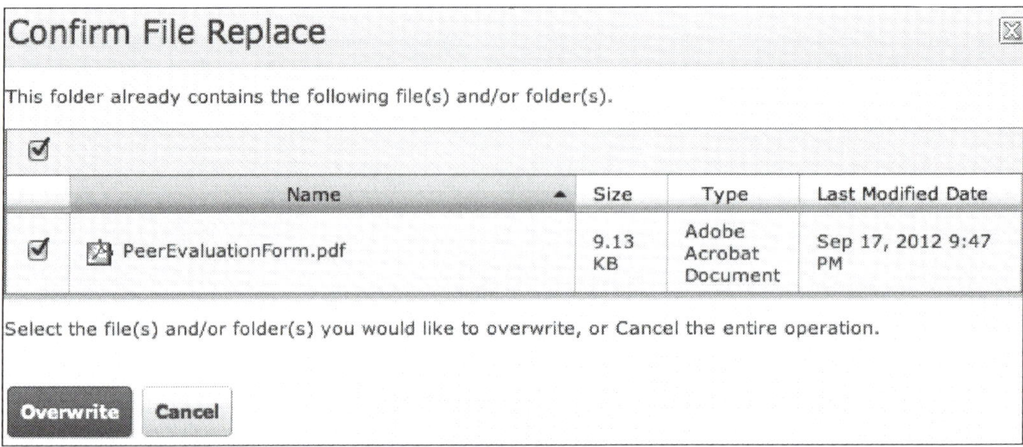

10. The **Modified Date** entry for the PDF should now reflect the current date and time.

How it works...

In a real course, some time would have passed between our original upload and the subsequent overwrite. You would have made some changes to the original document and re-saved it as a PDF. We've obviously simplified the process here by uploading a file and immediately replacing it.

In order for this technique to work, the filenames for both versions of the file have to be exactly the same. You'll know you did everything correctly if you are prompted to replace the existing file. If you don't get that message, verify that that the updated file name matches the name of the file currently available in the course.

See also

▶ The *Uploading folders to batch create course content* recipe

Uploading folders to batch create course content

You're probably familiar with the **Add Content** button in the Content tool. Among other things, it allows us to upload new documents and link to them from inside the Content area of a course. While easy to use, the tool has limited functionality; it's only capable of uploading a single file at a time (in version 10.0). What about those situations when you need to upload many items at once? Luckily, the Learning Environment's File Manager tool can handle uploading multiple files as well as `.zip` archives!

Getting ready

You'll need to identify a few files from your computer that you'd like to upload to your course. To make everything easier to find, go ahead and save a copy of the files in a folder on your desktop.

How to do it...

You can use the **Upload** icon in **File Manager** to upload multiple files at once. Unfortunately, you still need to browse and attach each file you want to upload one at a time. In this recipe, we will streamline the process by creating a **.zip** folder containing several PDF documents. We'll then upload the folder to our course, extract its contents, and create content topics pointing to each of the new files.

1. Locate the file folder containing the items you want to upload.

2. On your PC, right-click on the folder, select **Send To**, and click on **Compressed (zipped) Folder**. Mac users should right-click (or *Cmd* + click) and choose **Compress**.

3. Access your course and visit the **Content** tool.

4. Click the **Manage Files** tab.

5. Select the folder to which you want to upload the files in the folder tree on the left side of the page. I'm going to keep things simple and upload to the course's `root` folder.

6. Click on the **Upload** icon above the page's main content area. When prompted, click on the **Choose File** button and select the zipped folder saved to your computer's desktop. Click on the **Open** button.

7. Click on the **Upload** button.

8. Click on the newly uploaded file and choose **Unzip** from the context menu:

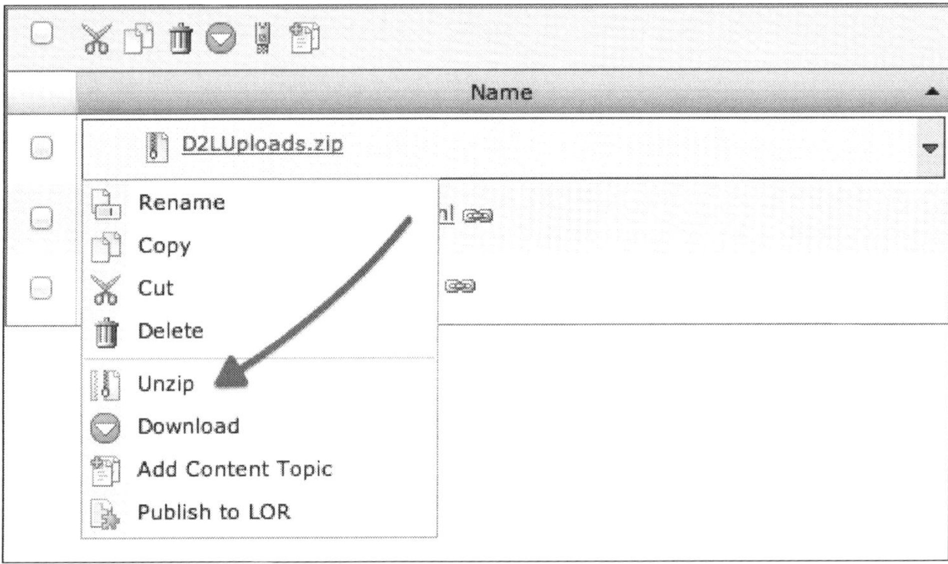

9. Let's go ahead and delete the original zipped folder since we now have an uncompressed version.

10. Click on the **.zip** folder and choose **Delete** from the drop-down context menu.

11. Let's take a look at the contents of the folder. Select the folder by clicking on it in either the folder tree or in the main panel.

12. Activate the checkboxes for each item in the folder.

13. Click on the **Add Content Topics** icon:

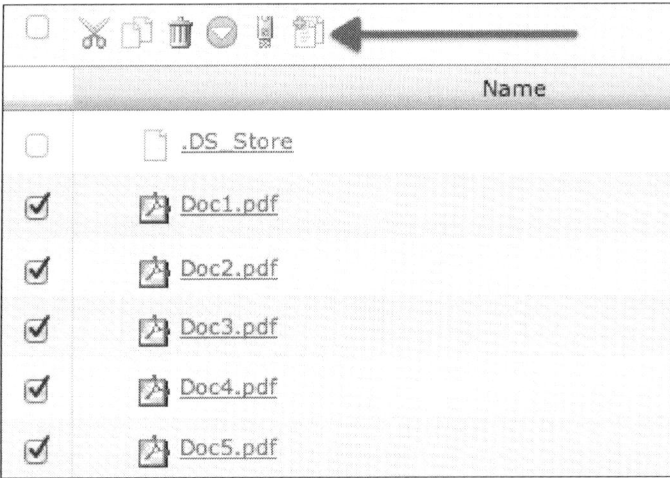

14. In the drop-down menu at the top of the page, choose an existing module in which we will place our new topics. To create a new module, click on the **add module** link.

15. Provide titles for each file in the **Topic Title** column. These are the titles displayed to students in the Content tool.

16. Click on the **Add** button.

17. Head back to the **Content** area. You should now see topics linking to each of the documents we just uploaded.

How it works...

We start off by creating a `.zip` folder containing all of the files we want to upload. Creating this archive helps us in a couple of ways. First, it allows us to select a single item during the upload process. If we hadn't created the `.zip` folder, we would have needed to use the **Add Another File** button and select each file separately:

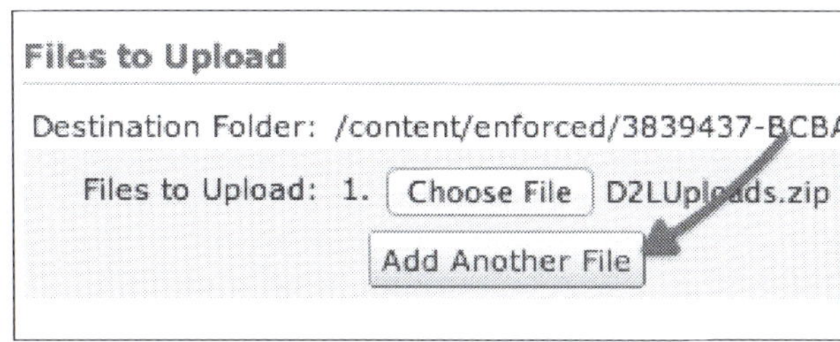

Once the folder has been successfully uploaded and extracted, it's a good idea to go ahead and delete the `.zip` folder, just as we did in this recipe. There's no reason to keep the compressed folder around since the files now exist in another location.

The file manager offers a handy way of batch creating content links to multiple course files at once. Select all of the items you want to link to and click on the **Add Content Topics** icon to create the links. You may have noticed that we were only able to enter one module in step 14, so keep that in mind when selecting the items. To create topics in multiple items, you'd need to complete steps 12-16 multiple times.

See also

▶ The *Updating course files without deleting the original topics* recipe

Adding content from the Learning Object Repository

You probably work with a lot of talented individuals at your organization, and I bet there are times when you'd love to collaborate with other instructors to create content for your Desire2Learn Learning Suite course. You probably don't, however, want to add all of your colleagues to each of your courses. If your school uses Desire2Learn's Learning Object Repository, or LOR, you can easily share items, content, assessments, and more from your courses with other uses at your school. In addition, you can search the LOR for existing content submitted by other instructors and easily add shared objects to your own course.

Getting ready

To complete this recipe, you need access to the Learning Object Repository. Ideally, your school's LOR will also have some content that you want to use in your course.

How to do it...

In this recipe, we'll learn how to browse the LOR and add content you find to your own course.

1. Access your course and navigate to the **Content** area.

2. Click on the **Add Content** button. Then, choose the **Add Learning Object** option from the drop-down list.

3. Search for content by typing a keyword or two in the **Search For** field and clicking on the **Search** button. If you don't see anything that matches your query, click on **Browse** and then click on the **Browse All** icon.

4. Once you've found an object you want to add, check the circle to the left of the object. Then, click on the **Next** button.

5. Let's select **Create a Dynamic Link to object from Content** option, and click on the **Next** button.

6. Choose a module in which you would like to place the object in the **Parent Module** drop-down list, or click on the **add module** link to create a new one.

7. Click on the **Create Link** button.

How it works...

We can link to LOR content in a few different ways. In this recipe, we create a dynamic link to our content, which means that if the object is modified in the LOR, it will be also be updated in our course. With this option, however, we don't have the ability to customize the content ourselves. If you need the ability to edit the object, one of the other options might make more sense.

Creating a Locked Link to an item in the LOR locks the document in your course to the current version of the object in the LOR. With this option, we still don't get the ability to edit the object, but we don't have to worry about it changing either. When you do anticipate needing to edit the object, the **Import Into Content** option will be the best choice. Rather than linking to the LOR, the object is downloaded and added to the current course offering when this option is checked.

There's more...

So far, we've learned how to search a specific institution's LOR. If configured by your D2L administrator(s), you can also search external repositories.

Searching federated resources

In the **Search Repository** window, click on the **Show Search Options** link. You can select other repositories by placing checks next to items displayed in the **Federated Resources** area.

Search For: Search

Hide Search Options

Repositories: ☑LOR_PSTCC

Federated Resources: ☑MERLOT

If you add objects from federated resources, you won't be presented with the same linking options as for items contained in a local LOR. Instead, the system will create a quicklink from your course's content area to the external website. If you use this option, make sure to periodically check the quicklink's URL.

Using Google Docs to allow multiple download formats

In this recipe, we'll upload a PowerPoint presentation to Google Docs and share it with students in your Desire2Learn Learning Environment course. By uploading Microsoft Word, PowerPoint, and Excel files to Google Docs and converting them to the service's own document formats, we gain some useful functionality that you may find beneficial to your online students. For example, students will be able to download our PowerPoint presentation in multiple formats including PowerPoint (`.pptx`) and PDF. In addition, students viewing the document can collaborate in real-time using Google's built-in chat functionality. Students aren't the only ones who benefit, however. You'll find that Google Docs retains document formatting better than Desire2Learn Learning Environment's own HTML editor, and the editing interface is more similar to the tools you're probably already using.

Getting ready

We will be uploading a PowerPoint presentation to Google Docs, so you'll need a Google account along with at least one presentation to work with. Although we are using a PowerPoint presentation in our example, the same basic process detailed in the following section would also work for word processing documents and spreadsheets. So, feel free to use one of those formats instead if you prefer.

How to do it...

Google Docs provides a choice between several privacy options for documents uploaded to the service. We're going to allow anyone with a link to view the document so that students don't need to create or remember an additional login username and password to gain access to it.

1. Open your web browser and navigate to the following URL: `www.docs.google.com`.

2. If prompted, go ahead and log in to your Google account.

3. Now, click on the **Upload** icon in the left column. Since we're uploading a single presentation at this time, let's choose the **Files** option.

4. Select the presentation you want to upload, and click on the **Open** button.

5. In the **Upload Settings** window, make sure the option to convert documents to the corresponding Google Docs format is checked:

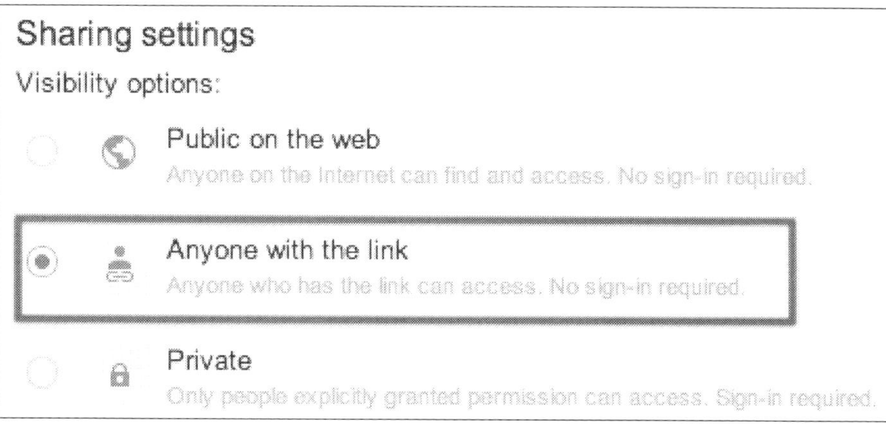

6. Let's view the document by clicking on it. The document, along with some editing options, should now fill the screen. Locate the **Share** button in the top-right corner of the screen. Go ahead and click on it to open **Sharing Settings**.

7. The presentation is probably set to **Private** by default. This won't work, since we're going to link to it from within our course. So, click on the **Change** link, and select **Anyone with the link**:

8. Click on **Save**.

9. Select the URL from the **Link to share** text field and copy it to you clipboard using the keyboard shortcut *Ctrl + C* or *Cmd + C* (Mac).

10. Click on **Done**.

11. In another tab, access your online course and navigate to the **Content** tool.

12. Let's create a new topic using the **New Topic** button. Since we're linking to an external site, choose the **Quicklink** option on the next screen.

13. Provide a title and choose a module for the new topic. Then, paste the address we just copied for the Google document into the URL text field using the keyboard shortcut *Ctrl + V* or *Cmd + V* (Mac).

14. Make sure the **Preview/view the content topic in a new window or tab** option is checked and click on the **Save** button.

How it works...

Google Docs works best in modern browsers such as Google Chrome. Most features will work in all current browsers, but you definitely don't want to access the site using old versions of Internet Explorer. If you're a Google Drive user, you're probably also aware of the desktop application that syncs local documents with those stored in the Cloud. We've chosen not to use that application here, since we need access to the website to set sharing options and copy the document's URL.

By default, files stored in Google Docs are kept private when created. In order to allow students to access the files, we changed the privacy settings to allow anyone with a link to view it. The file would now be accessible via a link from your course, but it still wouldn't appear in search engine results.

Once the sharing link is created, we just need to copy from Google and paste it in our Desire2Learn Learning Environment course. In this example, we created a quick link in the content area, but we could have easily created a news item or linked to the document from the discussion tool. You can return to the file at any time to update its content or adjust sharing settings.

There's more...

So far, we've looked at how an instructor adds content from Google Docs to a Desire2Learn Learning Environment course, but we haven't discussed the student experience yet. Let's take a quick look now.

Visitors can view the presentation using the slide navigator on the left side of the screen or by pressing the **Start presentation** button. One of the best features of Google Drive is the built-in chat window on the right side of the page. Visitors can see who else is viewing the document and interact with them using the chat area:

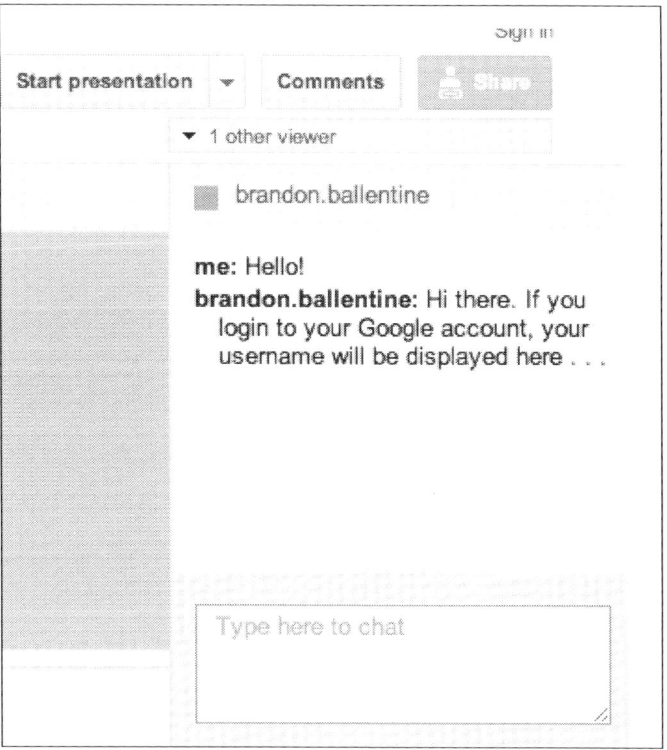

By accessing the **File** menu, students can download the presentation in a number of different formats:

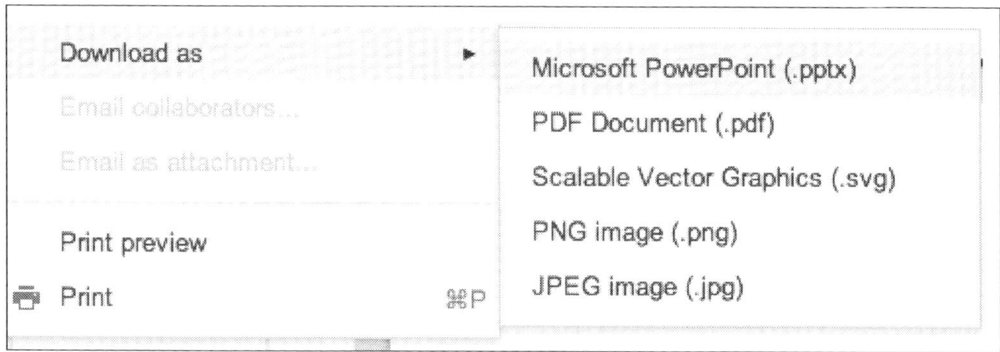

See also

- The *Getting existing Microsoft Word documents into your course* and *Working with PowerPoint presentations* recipes

4
Working with Multimedia

In this chapter, we will cover the following recipes:

- Finding Creative Commons licensed images
- Embedding web videos
- Working with YouTube playlists
- Recording how-to videos with Jing
- Recording and editing videos with YouTube
- Creating audio files using Audacity

Introduction

The consumption of online videos has skyrocketed in the past few years. In December 2011, 182 million U.S. Internet users watched a total of 43.5 billion videos. YouTube, the most popular online video site, reports that users upload an hour of video to the site each second and view 4 billion videos globally each day. As videos and other media continue to become a more important part of our students' lives outside the classroom, it only makes sense to think of ways to use the ubiquitous technology to our advantage in the classroom. Images, audio files, and streaming videos can be a great way of explaining difficult concepts and addressing students' various learning styles.

In this chapter, we will discuss some simple tools for working with multimedia in a Desire2Learn Learning Suite course. We'll start off by discussing how to find and embed Creative Commons licensed images. Next, we will learn how to use embed codes from video sites, such as YouTube, Vimeo, and Screencast.com, to add existing videos in our online courses. We will also take a look at how to group related YouTube videos together using playlists. In other recipes, we'll tackle media creation using several different online services and desktop apps.

You'll notice that in most of these recipes, we use external sites to actually host our media files, adding the content to Desire2Learn Learning Suite course through the use of embed code. This method allows us to take advantage of the infrastructure of these external sites and still makes the content available in our online courses. When possible, it's always a good idea to host audio and video files on servers designed to deliver streaming content to users. Doing so makes the content easier to view on a variety of different devices with varying connection speeds.

Finding Creative Commons licensed images

Adding images you find on the web to your documents and presentations is usually a fairly simple task. In most cases, you can simply right-click on an image in your web browser to save it to your computer for later use (or even click and drag to a location on your desktop in some browsers). However, you can run into potential copyright issues if you aren't careful. Many images you discover online are copyrighted by the individuals who created the work. By using their work in your own documents, you may be violating copyright law. Although legislation, such as the TEACH Act in the United States, is designed to make it easier to use copyrighted work in educational settings, we're going to bypass the problem altogether and search only for images that have been licensed for public use.

Getting ready

We don't need anything special to complete this recipe; a web browser and access to a Desire2Learn Learning Suite course should do the trick.

How to do it...

We're going to use Google's **Advanced Image Search** feature to find images that are designated with a **Creative Commons** (**CC**) license. CC licenses allow content creators to retain some rights, while still allowing others to benefit from the work by using, sharing, or even modifying the original work. We will learn more about the variety of CC licenses a little later in this recipe.

1. Open your web browser and navigate to `www.google.com/images`.

2. Enter a search term in the text field and click on the magnifying glass icon. I'm going to search for the keyword "cells", but feel free to use a term from your own subject area if you'd like.

3. Click on the gear icon in the top right corner of the screen. Then, click on the **Advanced Search** link in the menu that appears:

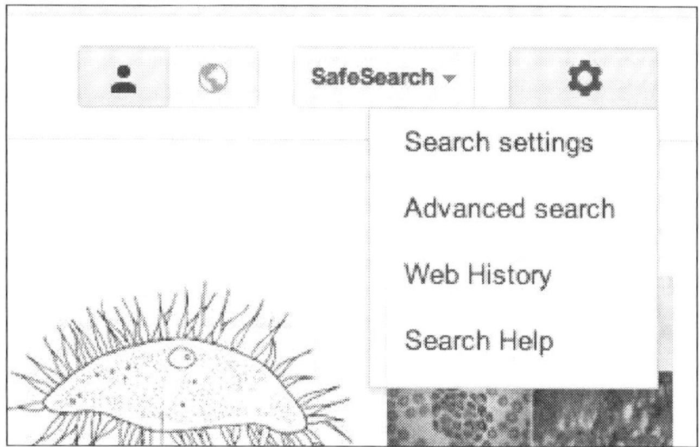

4. Scroll to the bottom of the page and click on the **usage rights** drop-down menu. Select **free to use or share**. Then, click on the **Advanced Search** button at the bottom of the page:

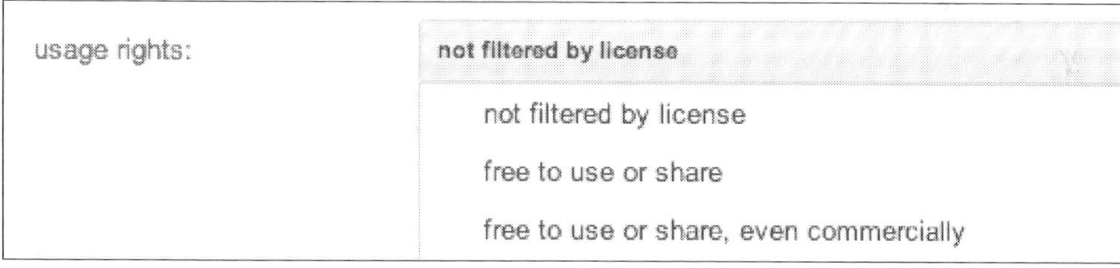

5. Click on the image to view additional details. Notice any usage information in the column to the right. Some images require attribution to the creator in order to use them. Click on the **Full-size image** link to display the image in its own window or tab.

6. Right-click on the image and choose **Save Image As**. In the dialog box that appears, choose a destination for the image and click on **Save**.

The wording may be slightly different in some browsers. Just look for the option that allows you to save the image.

7. Access your Desire2Learn Learning Suite course, and navigate to the **Content** tool.

8. Create a new topic by clicking on the **Add Content** button and selecting the **New File** option.

9. Choose a module in which you will add this image. Provide a title, and go ahead and enter a bit of text.

10. Now, let's add our downloaded image. Click on the **Image** icon in the **Content** editor toolbar. Click on the **Choose File** button in the pop-up window that appears:

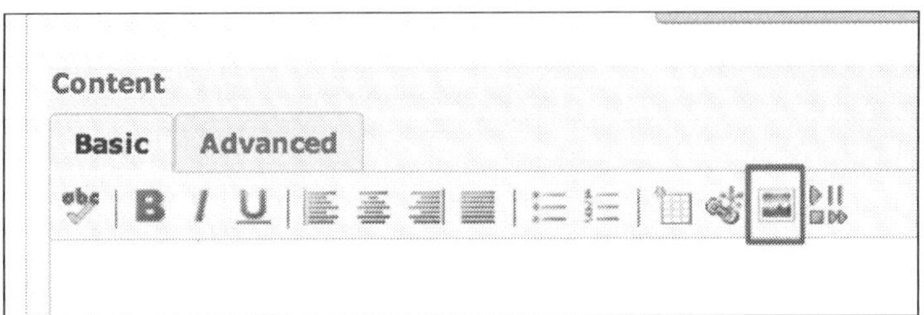

11. Locate the file and click on the **Open** button.

12. Finally, click on **Upload**. When prompted, provide some alternative text for students using screen readers. Depending on the resolution of the image, you may need to use an image editor, such as Adobe Photoshop, GIMP, or the online service PicMonkey, to reduce the file size. Take a look at the *Using your profile to add personality* recipe in *Chapter 2, Personalizing your D2L Site*, for more information.

13. Click on the icon in the lower-left corner of the HTML editor to edit the source code. Locate the `<img>` tag in your code. Then, place the following opening and closing `<figure>` and `<figcaption>` tags around it, as shown in the following code:

```
<figure>
   <img src="/content/enforced/xxreplace-with-your-
      codexxx/image1.png" alt="Alt Text for image goes
      here" title="Alt Text for image goes here" />
   <figcaption>
      Image by <a href="http://www.example.com>FirstName
         LastName</a>.
   </figcaption>
</figure>
```

14. Go ahead and replace the placeholder text with the actual first name, last name, and Web address for the image creator.

15. Click on the **Update** button when done.

16. Click on the on the **Save** button.

How it works...

You probably noticed that the list of available images dramatically decreased after performing our advanced search. That's expected, since we are limiting the results by images with a CC license. We also added a caption to our image and a link back to the creator's website. If you visit the CC website (`http://creativecommons.org/licenses`), then you'll see there are several different licenses available to content creators, each with different restrictions. Some licenses allow the work to be modified while others do not. Some also restrict use to non-commercial projects. One thing they all have in common is that they require the creator of the work to be properly credited. By linking to the licensor's website, we're meeting that obligation. Even if you're using an image that does not require attribution, it's a good habit to do so anyway. Not only is it the polite thing to do, but it can also be helpful if you need to re-download the image or find similar illustrations later on.

There's more...

Searching for CC licensed images is an option in most search engines and image hosting sites. Although the process may differ slightly, the same basic procedure should work. The popular image-sharing site Flickr, for example, displays a small **Advanced Search** link to the right of the **Search** field. Once selected, the option to limit search results to CC licensed images appears at the bottom of the page, much like we just saw in Google's image search utility:

@creative commons

Tip: Find content with a Creative Commons license. Learn more...

☑ Only search within **Creative Commons**-licensed content

☐ Find content to use commercially
☐ Find content to modify, adapt, or build upon

See also

▶ The *Using your profile to add personality* recipe in *Chapter 2, Personalizing Your Course*

Embedding web videos

Video sharing sites, such as YouTube, contain videos on just about any topic you can imagine. In this recipe, we'll use the **Insert Stuff** dialog to embed videos hosted on external sites in your Desire2Learn Learning Suite course.

Getting ready

In order to complete this recipe, your role in the current course needs permission to access the YouTube search tool in the Insert Stuff dialog.

How to do it...

We will use the built-in functionality of the Insert Stuff dialog to search for and embed videos from YouTube without ever having to leave your course. For other sites, such as Hulu or Vimeo, we'll need to copy and paste the embed codes from the sites into the HTML editor.

1. Access your course and navigate to the **Content** tool.

2. Click on the **Add Content** button. Then, select the **New File** option.

3. Assign the topic to an existing module within the course or create a new one using the **New Module** link.

4. Provide a title. Then, position your cursor inside the WYSIWYG editor.

5. Let's create a heading for the page and assign it the **Heading 1** style from the drop-down menu.

6. Compose a few sentences introducing the video. Press the *Return* key to move the cursor to a new line.

7. Click on the **Insert Stuff** icon.

8. Choose the **YouTube** option and enter a search term in the text field. Click on the **Search** button.

9. Preview any of the videos in a pop-up window or on YouTube by hovering over the video thumbnail and choosing one of the available options that appear.

10. When you find a video that you'd like to use, select it by clicking anywhere in the row to the right of the thumbnail

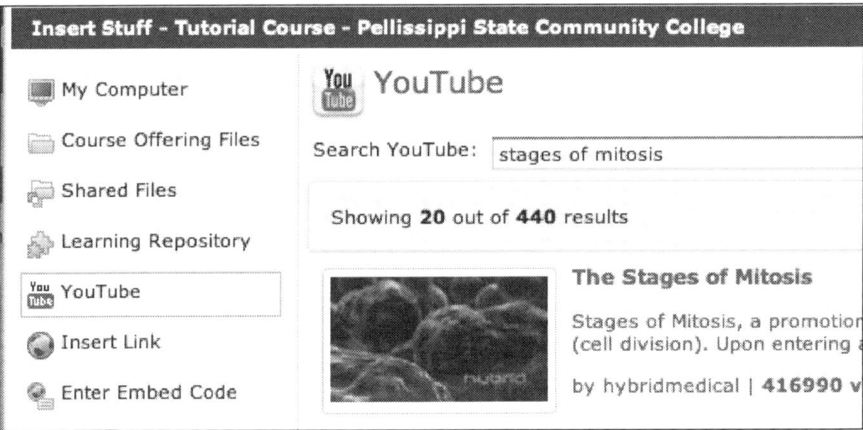

11. Click on the **Next** button. You should now see your video in the preview area.

12. Click on **Insert**.

13. Click on the **Save** button when you're finished editing the topic's content.

How it works...

Luckily, the WYSIWYG editor handles most of the work if you're embedding a YouTube video. We're only responsible for providing a search term when prompted and selecting the video we would like to use. Once we do that, the HTML editor automatically adds the correct embed code in the content area for us.

There's more...

We have to use a slightly different approach for embedding videos from other sites, such as Vimeo and Hulu. Instead of searching for content from within the Insert Stuff tool, we need to locate an embed code for the video on the external site and paste it in the **Enter Embed Code** section of the **Insert Stuff** dialog. The location of the embed code will differ depending on the site you're using, but you can usually find it by scanning the page for the words embed or share. Let's take a quick look at embedding content from Vimeo.

1. Locate a video you'd like to use at www.vimeo.com.

2. Click on the **Share** button in the upper-right corner of the video:

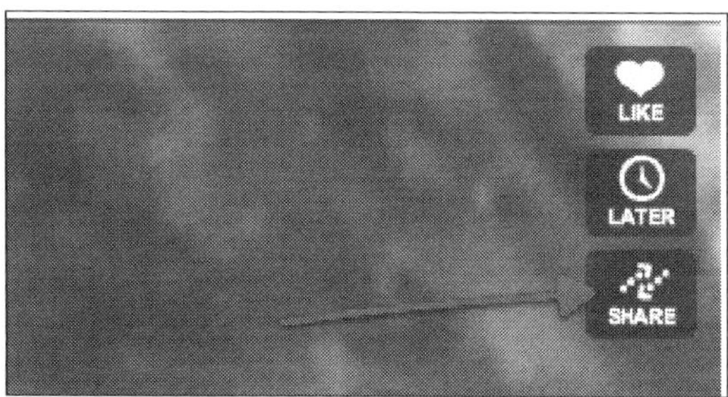

3. Select the embed code. Copy the code to your clipboard using the keyboard shortcut *Cmd + C* (Mac) or *Ctrl + C* (PC):

Embed

```
<iframe src="http://player.vimeo.com/video/83336437
title=0&amp;byline=0&amp;portrait=0&amp;color=ffffff"
width="500" height="281" frameborder="0"
webkitAllowFullScreen mozallowfullscreen
```

This is our embed code which supports iPad, iPhone, Flash and beyond.

4. Access your course and navigate to the **Content** tool.

5. Click on the **Add Content** button and choose the **New File** option.

6. Provide a title for the topic.

7. Click on the **Insert Stuff** icon in **HTML Editor** toolbar.

8. Click on the **Enter Embed Code** option and paste the code we just copied into the text area provided. Then, click on the **Next** button:

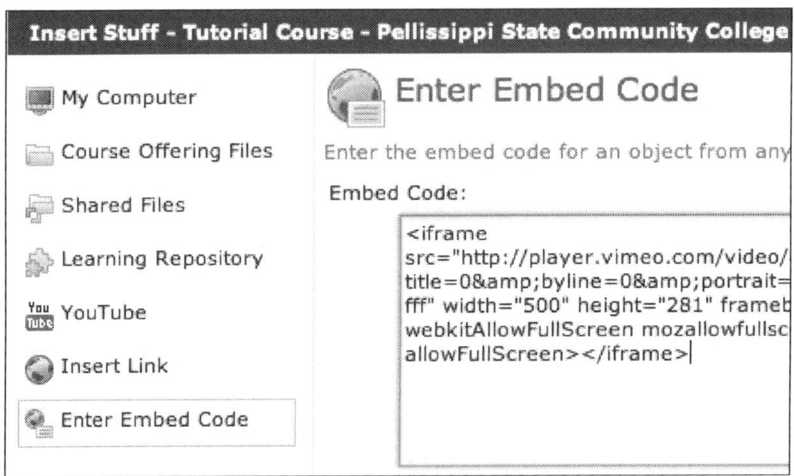

9. If presented with a **Content Blocked** message, check the **Always allow this page** option. Then, click on the **Allow** button:

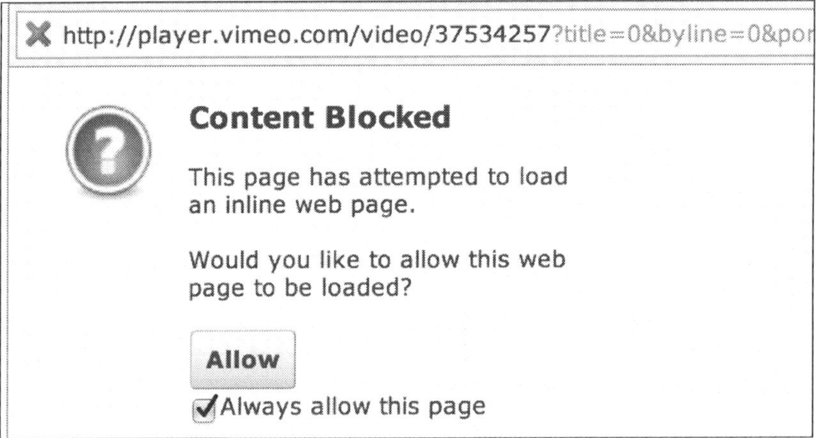

10. Click on the **Insert** button.

11. Save your work by clicking on the **Save and Close** button.

See also

▸ The *Recording how-to videos with Jing* , *Working with YouTube playlists*, and *Recording and editing videos with YouTube* recipes

Working with YouTube playlists

YouTube playlists are a collections of videos that play one after another in a specific order. Playlists are a great way to group related videos together, so that students don't need to visit multiple URLs to view a series of videos. In addition, once embedded in a course content page, you can easily edit the playlist from your YouTube account without needing to edit anything in your Desire2Learn Learning Suite course.

Getting ready

We're going to use YouTube's playlist editor to create our playlist. If you don't, go ahead and register for one before moving forward. After creating our playlist, we're going to add it to a **Content** page of a Learning Suite course. If you're unfamiliar with using embed codes, take a look at the previous recipe, *Embedding web videos*, for more detailed instructions.

How to do it...

1. Navigate to `http://www.youtube.com` and log in to your account.

2. Click on your name in the upper-right corner of the page and select the **Video Manager** option.

3. Click on the **Playlists** link in the left column.

4. Let's create playlist for our course by clicking on the **New Playlist** button:

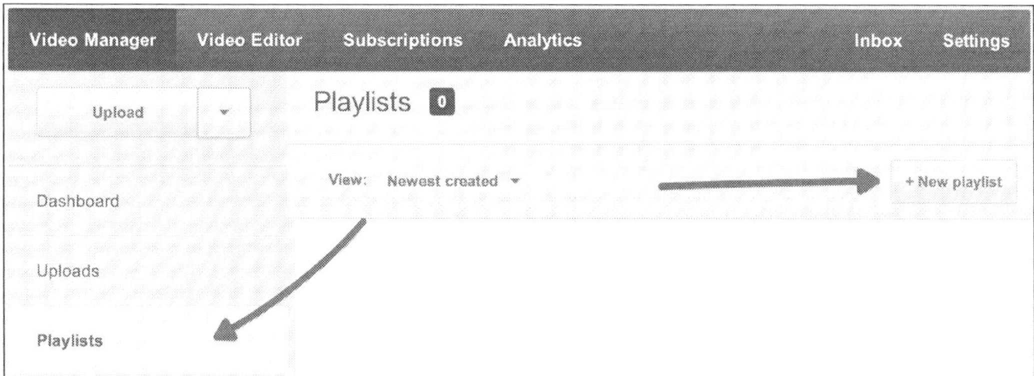

5. Provide a title and description for the playlist. Click on the **Create playlist** button.

6. Now we need to add some videos to our new playlist. Search YouTube for a video you'd like to add to the playlist. When you find one, click on the **Add to** button under the video player. Select the playlist you just created and add an additional note if you'd like. Repeat this process to add several more videos to the playlist

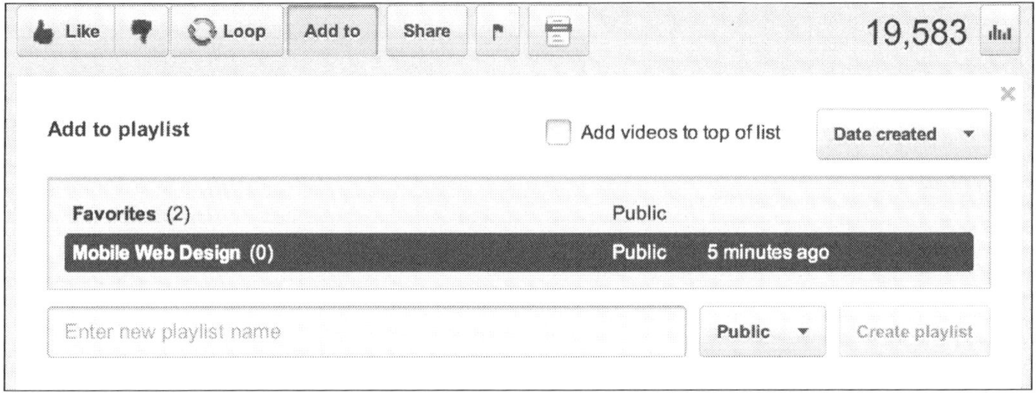

7. Let's head back to our playlist editor now. Access the **Video Manager** page and click on the **Playlists** link or just type `https://www.youtube.com/view_all_playlists` in your browser's address bar.

8. Click on the playlist's title. Then, click on the **Share** button at the top of the page:

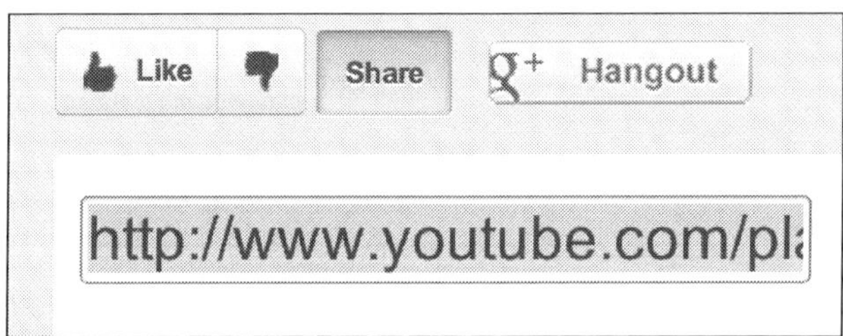

9. Copy the URL from the text field, open a new tab, and access the **Content** tool in one of your courses.

10. Create a new topic in which you want to embed the playlist. After providing a title, click on the **Insert Stuff** icon on the HTML editor.

11. Click the **Insert Link** option in the left column and paste the address you just copied from your YouTube page into the URL text field.

12. Click on the **Next** button. Add your video by clicking on the **Insert** button.

13. Don't forget to save your topic when finished.

How it works...

Once embedded within a Desire2Learn Learning Suite course, students can watch the entire playlist by pressing the play button in the video player. As one video finishes, the next one automatically begins. If needed, students can also navigate directly to specific videos by clicking on the playlist icon at the bottom of the player and selecting on one of the video thumbnails.

After creating and embedding a playlist, you can add additional videos to it or even change the order of the videos directly from your YouTube account; you don't need to generate a new embed code or edit anything inside your course. Rearrange existing videos by visiting the **Video Manager** page and clicking on the **Edit** button for the playlist you want to modify. Then click and drag videos to alter their order in the playlist.

You can also provide your own introductions to any of the playlist's videos by hovering over the thumbnail and clicking on the **Introduction** button. A pop-up window appears that allows you to either record your own video introduction using a webcam or to type your a short introduction material:

See also

- The *Embedding web videos* recipe

Recording how-to videos with Jing

Jing is a free, cross-platform application that you can use to create and share images and videos captured from your computer screen. It is made by **TechSmith**, a company that produces other screen capture and screencasting applications such as Snagit and Camtasia Studio. While the application doesn't have all of the bells and whistles of its paid counterparts, you'll probably find its feature set more than adequate for producing quick how-to videos.

In this recipe, we will create a short video that demonstrates an aspect of the Desire2Learn Learning Suite interface and embed it in a news item on your course homepage. **Short** is the keyword here. As with many free services, Jing does have a few limitations, and the one that you'll quickly encounter, if you aren't careful, is the time limit for captured video. Jing is limited to five-minute recordings. So, you'll either need to chunk larger topics into several smaller clips or invest in full-featured screencasting application such as Camtasia Studio.

Getting ready

Before we start, head over to `http://www.techsmith.com/jing.html` to download and install the most recent version of Jing for your operating system. We'll be posting our video to a free screencast.com account, but you don't need to create that account at this time. Jing will prompt us for login information when it's time to publish our work.

You're also going to need some type of computer microphone in order to capture audio for our project. In most cases, a laptop with a built-in microphone will work just fine, but you're welcome to use an external microphone or headset if you prefer. No matter what input device you choose, it's important to minimize background noise. You may not notice ambient sounds emitted by air conditioning units, audio e-mail notifications, or even fluorescent lights, but your viewers will definitely notice them in your recordings.

How to do it...

1. Access your course.

2. Launch the Jing application.

3. Hover over the Jing application in the corner of the computer screen. Click on the gear icon when it appears:

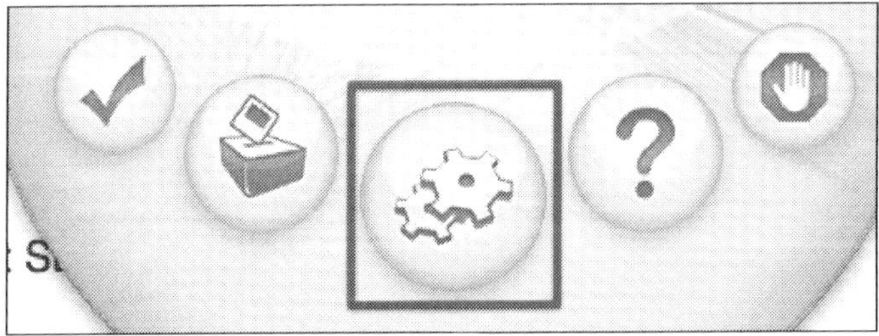

4. Click on the **Preferences** icon. Under the **Audio Device** heading, click on the **Select Device** button. Speak into the microphone and make sure that the correct input is selected:

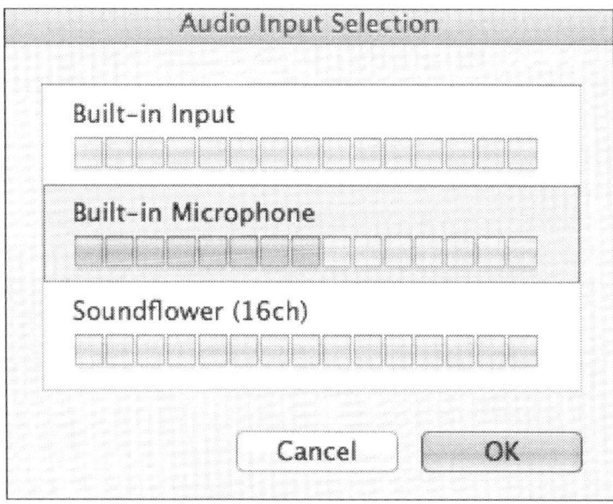

5. Click on the **OK** button. Then, click on the **Done** (checkmark) button to return to the main app interface.

6. Hover over the application, and click on the crosshair icon. Now, position your cursor over the browser window and left-click to select the recording area. The rest of the screen should dim to indicate the current recording region.

7. When you're ready to record, click on the **Capture a Video** icon (second from the left).

8. After the countdown completes, take a few minutes to record an introduction to your course, showing students where to look for assignments, how to check their grades, and so on. Click on the **Finish** button when you're done creating your video.

9. The video won't do a lot of good if it stays on your PC, so let's publish it to the Web. Replace the default name for the video with a more descriptive one and click on the **Share via Screencast.com** button:

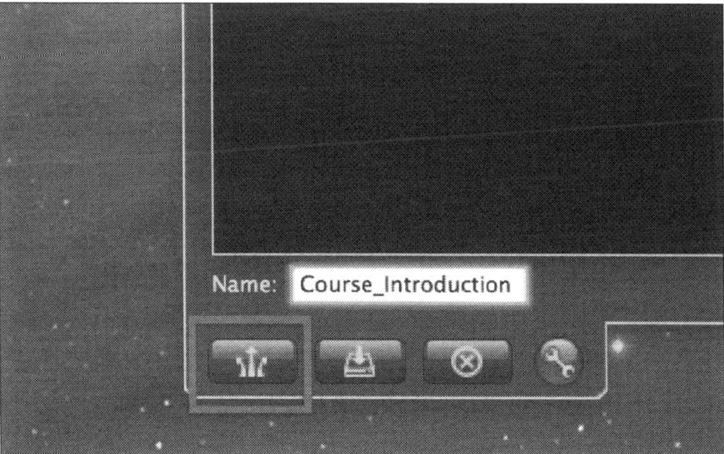

10. If you don't already have a Screencast.com account, select the **Create a new account** radio button. Enter values for **E-mail**, **Display Name**, and **Password** for the account. Then, click on **Create**:

11. Your upload should start after the account creation process is complete. Once you receive a notification that the upload is complete, open another tab in your browser and go `www.screencast.com`.

12. Let's go ahead and log in to the site using the credentials we supplied in step 10.

13. Make sure the **All items** option is selected in the **Show me** section. Check the box next to the video in the main content area. Then, click on the **Share** button:

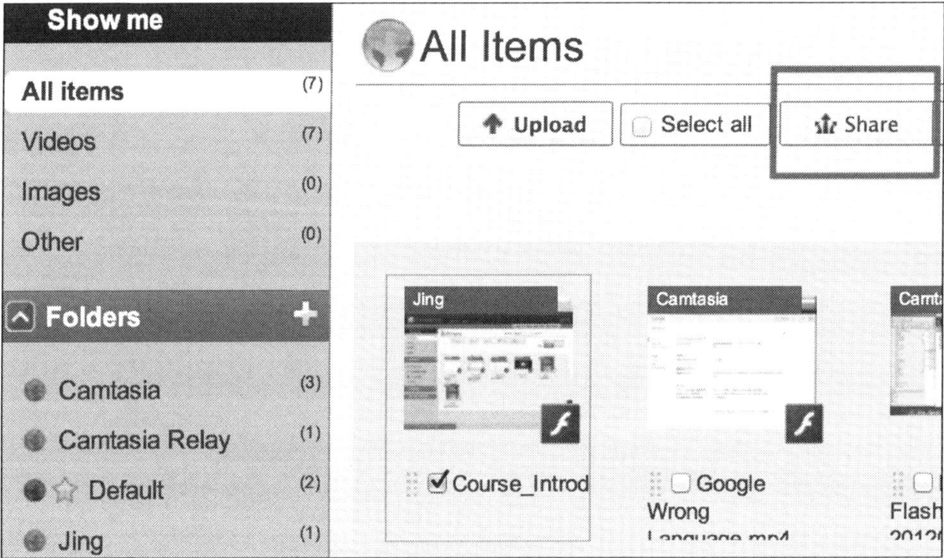

14. Position your cursor in the text field under the **Embed on your page** heading. Copy the text to your clipboard using the keyboard shortcut *Ctrl + C*.

15. Now, return to your course homepage, activate the News context menu, and select the **New News Item** option.

16. Provide a headline for the new item. Then position your cursor in the HTML editor and click on the **Insert Stuff** icon.

17. Choose the **Enter Embed Code** option and paste the code into the text area to the right:

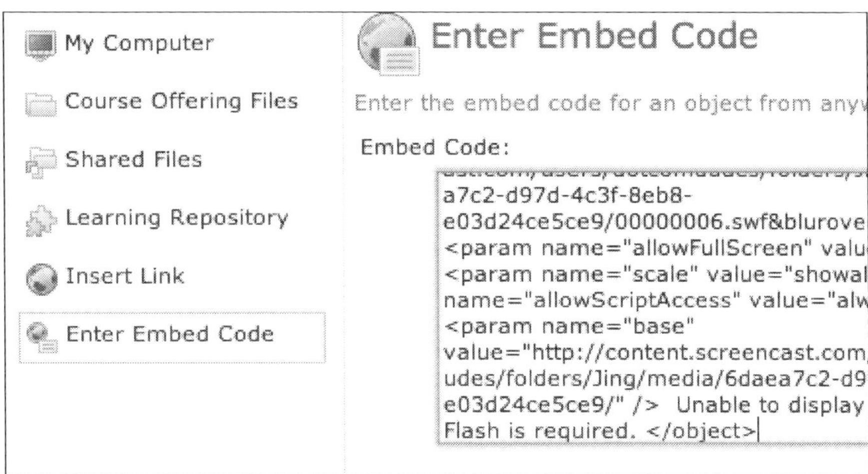

18. Click on the **Next** button and then on the **Insert** button.

19. Save the news item by clicking on the **Publish** button. Let's verify that everything works correctly by navigating back to the course homepage. You should see your video embedded on the page.

How it works...

After installing and launching the application, your next step is to verify that your microphone is configured correctly. Nothing is worse than finishing a perfect recording only to realize that no audio was captured! Then, select your recording area. Although we chose the entire browser window in this recipe, you can select a custom area by left-clicking and dragging a rectangle anywhere on the computer screen.

By default, Jing is configured to upload to screencast.com, a video and image hosting site created by the company that makes Jing. We created a free account in order to share our video, but the service also offers a paid **Pro account** with more storage and a higher bandwidth allowance. Once you upload a video, simply log in to the site and grab the embed code to use in your Desire2Learn Learning Suite course. Although we chose the third option (embed on your own site) in this example, we could have also chosen to copy the video's URL or embed a link using the other two options. If you prefer not to use screencast.com to host your videos, you can also save a `.swf` media file to your computer that you can upload to a service of your choice.

See also

▶   The *Embedding web videos* and *Recording and editing videos with YouTube* recipes

Recording and editing videos with YouTube

In the past, recording and editing digital video typically involved expensive hardware and complex software. Things have changed a lot in the past few years, and now it's possible to capture high quality video on mobile phones or using inexpensive webcams and easily upload content to sites such as YouTube. In this recipe, we'll use two of YouTube's features, the **webcam recorder** and **online video editor**, to create a quick **Instructor Introduction** video to place on your course homepage.

Getting ready

In order to complete this recipe, you're going to need a YouTube account, along with a webcam and microphone for your computer. In addition, I highly recommend taking a few minutes to draft a script for your video. Working from a script helps focus your presentation. In addition, we'll use the script at the end of the recipe when creating closed captions for our video. While you're welcome to compose the transcript after recording, I find it easier to do so ahead of time. Make sure to save your transcript as a `.txt` document.

You'll also need the **Flash plugin** installed for the browser of your choice. You'll be prompted to download and install Flash if you don't already have it (chances are you do) when we begin recording.

How to do it...

We're going to be using YouTube's built-in webcam recorder to create our video introduction; however, you can use the same basic procedure to post and edit videos created from another source such as iMovie, Windows Movie Maker, Adobe Premiere, or just about any other video editing application.

1. Start out by opening your web browser, navigating to www.youtube.com, and logging into your account.

2. Click on the **Upload** link near the top-right corner of the page.

3. Click on the **Record from webcam** button:

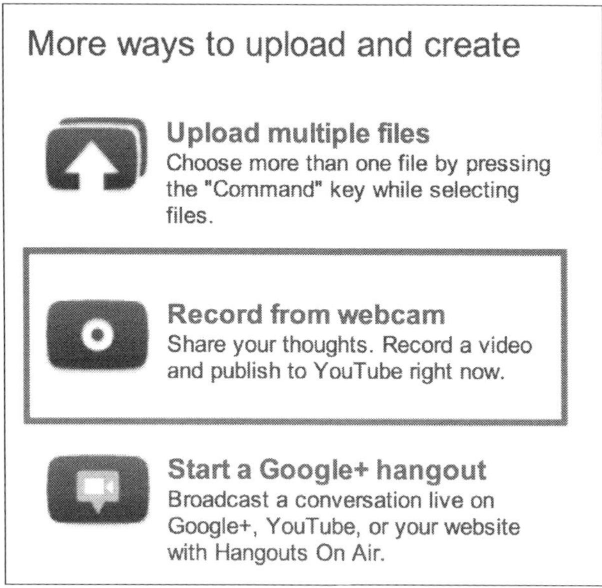

4. Select the **Allow** radio button to grant YouTube access to your computer's webcam and microphone. Click on **Close** once you see yourself in the preview window.

5. Click on the **Record** button and work your way through your introductory script.

6. Once you're done, click on the **Stop** button in the lower-left corner of the preview window. Let's go ahead and make sure everything looks good by clicking on the **Preview** button.

7. After the preview completes, go ahead and press the **Publish** button to post the recording to your YouTube account.

8. After the upload completes, you're directed to a page where you can enter a title and description for the video, set the privacy level, and more. Go ahead and take a few minutes to complete as much (or as little) of that information as you like.

9. Access the drop-down menu under your account name in the upper-right corner of the browser window and choose the **Video Manager** option.

10. Locate the video you just uploaded, then access the drop-down menu next to the **Edit** button and choose the **Captions** option.

11. Click on the **Add New Captions or Transcript** button.

12. Select the **Transcript** radio button. Then, click on the **Choose File** button to locate the transcript file on your local computer:

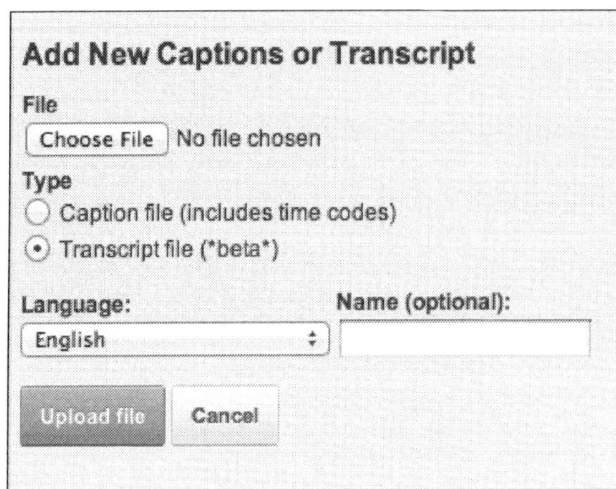

13. Click on the **Upload file** button to finish the process.
14. You can embed the YouTube video in your Desire2Learn Learning Suite course using the steps in the *Embedding web videos* recipe from earlier in this chapter.

How it works...

We used a webcam and microphone and YouTube's built-in recording functionality to create our course introduction. You probably noticed the option to upload an existing video. If you're comfortable using a more full-featured video editor, such as iMovie or Moviemaker, then you can definitely do so. After exporting the video from the external editor, you would just need to upload it to YouTube.

Once we have captured our video and published it to YouTube, we access the Video Manager area to add a transcript for our creation. Although still in beta, this tool does a fantastic job of matching the text from the uploaded transcript file with the recorded audio to create a closed caption file.

There's more...

YouTube now offers a simple, web-based video editor available at `www.youtube.com/editor`. Although not as powerful as many desktop video editors, the service does allow you to quickly trim and combine clips, add transitions, and create titles. When you access the online editor, you will see a clip bin in the upper-left corner, which is filled with all of the videos you've uploaded to the service. To create a new project, drag videos from the bin and drop them in the timeline area. You can also rearrange clips by dragging and dropping them to new positions in the timeline.

Additional resources

In addition to its own online editor, YouTube allows you to connect to other web-based video editing sites with more sophisticated editing tools. To see what services are available, navigate to `www.youtube.com/create`. You can learn more about any of the third-party services listed on the page by clicking on the service's title:

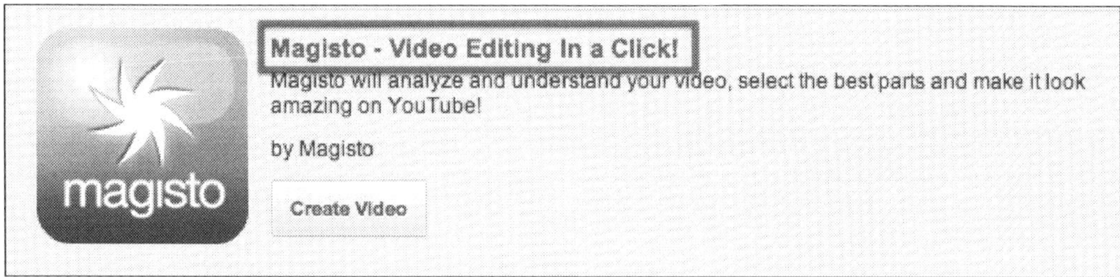

For the adventurous, YouTube also maintains several beta services, some of which may be useful in your online class. The Video Questions editor, for example, allows you to display multiple-choice questions over your videos to create a more engaging user experience. Keep in mind that if you decide to use any of these experiments, they may disappear at any point. To see the current list of services, log in to your YouTube account and navigate to `http://www.youtube.com/testtube`. Then, click on the **Try it out** link to activate a service for your account:

See also

▸ The *Embedding web videos* and *Recording how-to videos with Jing* recipes

Creating audio files with Audacity

Audacity is a free, open-source application available for Windows, Mac, and Linux operating systems. It's packed with all sorts of features that you can use to create professional sounding audio files. In this recipe, we'll use Audacity to capture a voice recording and export an MP3 suitable for sharing in your online course. We'll then use Google's Audio Player to embed the file in a news item in our online course.

If you've explored Desire2Learn Learning Suite's HTML editor, you may have noticed that there's already a tool for uploading and displaying an audio file. The system's native audio player, however, offers a bad experience for students. I recommend making use of some sort of third-party audio player. We're going to be using the player used in Google Reader, but feel free to use any other script with which you are familiar.

I'll be using Audacity 2.0 for the Mac OS in the screenshots to follow, but the interface is very similar for other operating systems. Audacity has a great Quick Start guide and a comprehensive manual accessible from within the program, so feel free to take a look at those recourses if you have any questions about your particular version of the app.

Getting ready

In order to complete this recipe, you're going to need Audacity, available at `http://audacity.sourceforge.net/`, installed on your computer. You're also going to need either a computer with a built-in microphone or access to an external microphone.

How to do it...

We're going to be exporting our recording in the MP3 format. Due to software patents, the MP3 encoding software can't be distributed with the Audacity application, so you're going to need to download and install the **LAME MP3** encoder. Once installed, you can export files in the MP3 format from within the program. For information on the plugin and how to install it, visit the **downloads** page for your operating system, `http://audacity.sourceforge.net/download/` and click on the link under the **Optional Downloads** header.

1. Launch Audacity and make sure your microphone is plugged in (if you're not using a built-in microphone).

2. In the **File** menu, click on **New** to start a new project. Then, choose **File | Save As**. Provide a name for the project, and choose a location on your computer to save your work.

3. Let's click on the red **Record** button to start a recording. Go ahead and talk for a few minutes. When finished, click on the yellow **Stop** button to complete the recording:

4. From the **File** menu, click on **Export**. Select a location to save your recording and select **MP3 Files** from the **Format** drop-down menu.

5. Click on the **Save** button.

6. Enter an artist name and title for our track. Then, click on **OK**:

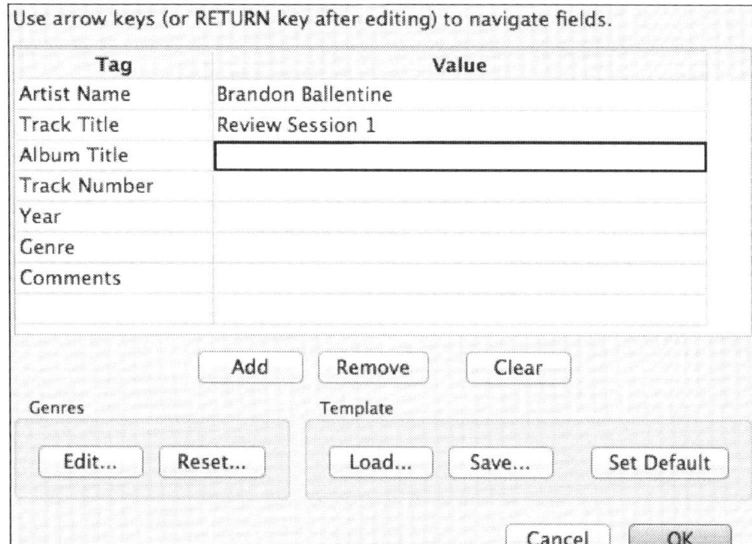

7. Access your Desire2Learn Learning Suite course and head to the **Manage Files** area, which can be accessed from either links in the **Content** tool or under **Edit Course**.

8. Click on the **Upload** icon. Then, click on the **Choose File** button and locate the MP3 file on your computer. Once selected, upload the file by clicking on the **Open** button followed by the **Upload** button.

9. Navigate back to the course's **Content** area. Create a new topic by clicking on the **Add Content** button and selecting the **New File** option. Go ahead and provide a title for the item. Then, select a module from the drop-down list.

10. Position your cursor in the HTML editor. Click on the icon to create a quicklink.

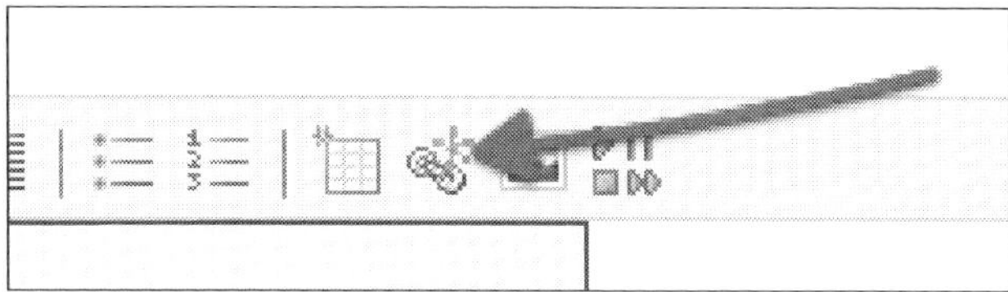

11. Select the **Course File** option in the **Category** drop-down list.

12. Click on the **Add a File** button, select the MP3 we just uploaded, and click on the **Select File** button. For **Link Caption**, type `Download Audio File`. Click on the **Insert** button.

13. Click on the small icon in the lower-left corner to switch to the HTML source view:

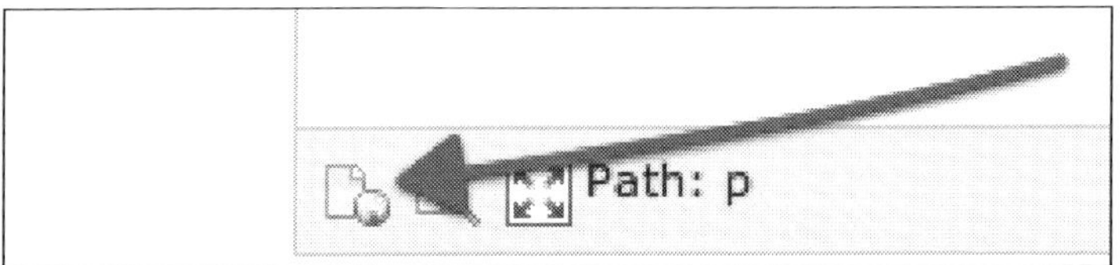

14. Paste the following code after the quick link but before the `</body>` tag:

```
<embed type="application/x-shockwave-flash"
   wmode="transparent" src="http://www.google.com/reader
   /ui/3523697345-audio-player.swf?audioUrl=[MP3_file]"
   height="27" width="320"></embed>
```

15. We're going to need to replace the MP3 placeholder with the URL for the file we uploaded. Take a look at the following screenshot. Copy the value for **Field** and paste it in place of the **[MP3_file]** text:

```
<!DOCTYPE html PUBLIC "-//W3C//DTD XHTML 1.0 Transitional//EN"
"http://www.w3.org/TR/xhtml1/DTD/xhtml1-transitional.dtd">
<html>
<head>
</head>
<body>
<p><a href="/d2l/common/dialogs/quickLink/quickLink.d2l?ou=
{orgUnitId}&amp;type=coursefile&amp;fileId=SampleRecording.mp3" target="_self">Download Audi
File</a></p>


<embed type="application/x-shockwave-flash" wmode="transparent"
src="http://www.google.com/reader/ui/3523697345-audio-player.swf?audioUrl=[MP3_file]"
height="27" width="320"></embed>
</body>
</html>
```

16. Click on the **Update** button. Then, save the content item by clicking on the **Save** button.

How it works...

We start by creating a voice recording in Audacity. Although our example is very simple one track and no background audio Audacity is capable of much more sophisticated editing. Feel free to experiment with the editor to see what else you can do. Audacity's Quick Start guide is a great place to look for additional information. You may have noticed the file we saved to the desktop at the beginning of the recipe had a `.aup` extension. Files with this extension are Audacity projects, which can be opened again and edited at a later date. These files, however, cannot be shared with others. That's why we export our recording as an MP3, a highly compressed file that can be shared with others.

After exporting an audio file, we upload it to the Learning Suite by visiting the Manage Content area of our course. We then create a quicklink in the content area to allow students to download the recording. We use the file's URL in Google's Audio Player code to create a working player on the page.

There's more...

At some point, you may want to add some background audio to your recordings. Some desktop audio-editing applications, such as Apple's GarageBand, provide loops and sounds that you can use in your projects. However, most audio files you'll run across in traditional web searches will be copyrighted, preventing their legal use in your course. One website, **CCMixter** (`http://ccmixter.org/`), offers thousands of Creative Commons licensed audio tracks that you can download and use in your projects.

Diving into HTML Code

5

In this chapter, we will cover:

- ▶ Displaying external web content with frames
- ▶ Using CSS to style content
- ▶ Using Desire2Learn's accessible templates
- ▶ Creating mobile-friendly content

Introduction

The HTML editor, available in many of the Learning Suite's tools, allows you to create web content without having to learn to write or edit code. Using a "what you see is what you get" (WYSIWYG) interface similar to that of popular word-processing applications, you can create documents, activities, quiz questions, course announcements, and more. While you don't often need to view a page's HTML source when creating basic content and activities, there are times when working with a page's source code offers some real advantages over interacting solely with the traditional, WYSIWYG view. In this chapter, we will explore some of those situations.

We'll start the chapter by using frames to display external websites within your Desire2Learn Learning Suite course. This technique is especially useful when students need to access materials on several different sites or pages to complete an assignment or explore a topic. Instead of linking to each of these sites and sending students outside the learning environment, you can embed these resources within a single page in your course. Next, we will use **Cascading Style Sheets** (**CSS**) to quickly give our content a uniform look and feel. After exploring the basics of CSS, our next recipe builds on our knowledge and discusses how to use Desire2Learn's accessible templates to create webpages that look better and are easier to read. We finish the chapter by building a mobile-friendly page template using the principles of **Responsive Web Design**.

The recipes in this chapter are written for individuals with limited web development experience. However, I do assume that you have a general understanding of HTML and CSS. You're welcome to follow along even if you don't meet these prerequisites; the steps contain all of the code you need to complete each task. However, you may find it difficult to expand on the recipes or customize the code to meet the needs of your own courses. Luckily, the web is full of great resources for learning how to develop webpages. One of my favorites is the interactive tutorial website, `www.codecademy.com`.

Displaying external web content with frames

In an HTML document, `<iframe>` elements are used to display other documents or web pages within the current page. This is a great approach for times when you want to show content from several different web pages in one place, such as showcasing student work, comparing information from multiple reference sites, and more. Instead of providing links to each of the sites we want a student to visit, we use frames to display those sites together in a more accessible way. In this recipe, we will create an essay assignment, embed a couple of YouTube videos, and use an `<iframe>` tag to add content from another site.

Getting ready

You'll need a YouTube video and at least one URL to use as the source for the `<iframe>` element. In this example, I'll be creating a content item for *Eudora Welty's* "A Worn Path", but feel free to adjust the steps to match your own course requirements.

How to do it...

We're going to use frames to display a YouTube video and text from another external site in your Desire2Learn Learning Suite course. The steps we discuss in this section can be used to embed almost any type of content you'd like. I encourage you to experiment with other options after completing this recipe.

1. Access your course and navigate to the **Content** tool.
2. Click on the **Add Content** button and choose the **New File** option.
3. Let's go ahead and provide a title for our new topic and assign it to an existing module in the course. Then, take a couple of minutes to type out an introduction for the page.

4. In a separate tab, head to `www.youtube.com` and locate a video you'd like to embed on the page. I'll be using the video available at `http://www.youtube.com/watch?v=XVOYj9CQX1o`, but you're welcome to use one more appropriate for your course. Once you've selected a video, click on the **Share** button.

5. Click on the **Embed** button. Then, select the code that appears in the text area, copy it to your clipboard, and return to your course:

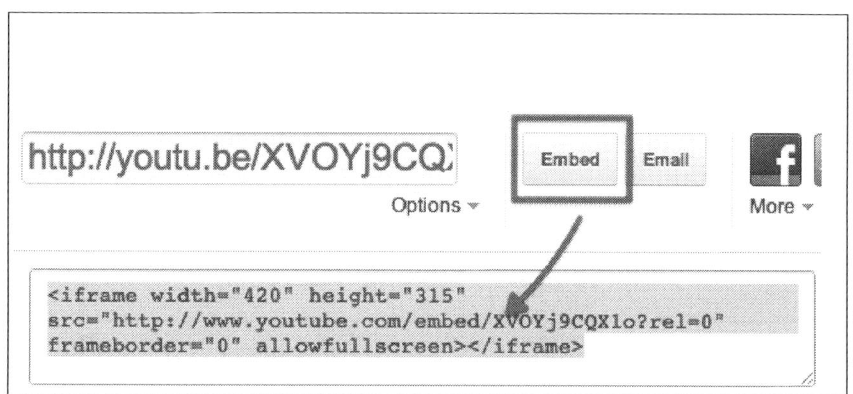

6. Access the HTML source view using the icon in the lower-left corner of the editor:

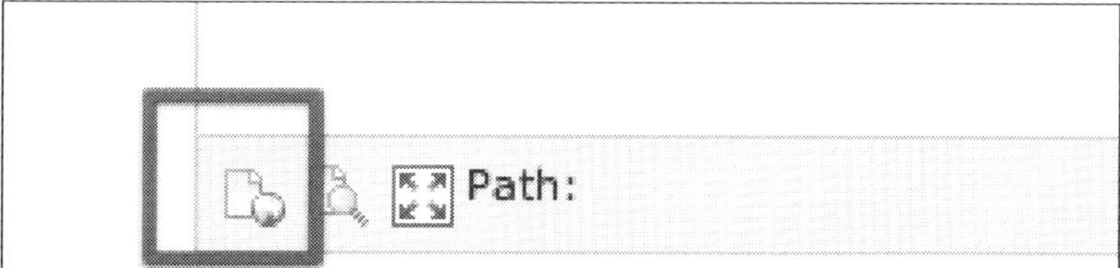

7. Position your cursor just above the `</body>` tag and paste the YouTube embed code.

8. While still in the HTML source view, type the following code after the closing `</iframe>` tag we just added:

```
<iframe width="800" height="600" src="http://www.theatlantic.com/
past/docs/issues/41feb/wornpath.htm" title="A Worn Path by Eudora
Welty"></iframe>
```

9. Click on the **Update** button.

10. Click on the **Save** button.

11. Use the **Preview** button at the top of the page to view the content we just created. You should see our introductory text, a YouTube video, and the content from the website we referenced in the `<iframe>` code:

A Worn Path

Instructions

Read "A Worn Path" by Eudora Welty and watch the video. After you are familiar with the story, visit the discussion forum and re[...] story's discussion questions.

A Worn Path

by Eudora Welty

.....

It was December—a bright frozen day in the early morning. Far out in the country there was an old Negro woman with her head tied in a red rag, coming along a path through the pinewoods. Her name was Phoenix Jackson. She was very old and small and she walked slowly in the dark pine shadows, moving a little from side to side in her steps, with the balanced heaviness and lightness of a pendulum in a grandfather clock. She carried a thin, small cane made from an umbrella, and with this she kept tapping the frozen earth in front of her. This made a grave and persistent noise in the still air that seemed meditative, like the chirping of a solitary little bird.

She wore a dark striped dress reaching down to her shoe tops, and an equally long apron of bleached sugar sacks, with a full pocket: all neat and tidy, but every time she took a step she might have fallen over her shoelaces, which dragged from her unlaced shoes. She looked straight ahead. Her eyes were blue with age. Her skin had a pattern all its own of numberless

How it works...

After creating our topic, we navigated to YouTube and copied the embed code for the video we want to use. If you look at the code we pasted, you'll see the `<iframe>` opening and closing tags. Did you notice the attributes between the tags? These are used to set the source, title, width, and height for the frame.

We used the YouTube embed code as a prototype for creating our own `<iframe>` tag in step 8. The `src=` attribute specifies the address of the page we are using as the source of the frame. Make sure that source is a valid URL, complete with the `http://` protocol, or the frame won't work correctly. The `width=` and `height=` attributes define in pixels how large the frame will appear on the page. If the original page is larger than the area you define here, the browser will add vertical or horizontal scroll bars.

As you can see, it is possible to have more than one frame per page. In our example, we have two frames, but you could include as many as you'd like. Just remember, however, that you are loading an entire external page in each frame, so a page with multiple frames may load more slowly than a regular page. Some sites prohibit their pages from being displayed in frames. If you set a frame's source to one of these sites, no content will appear. It's also important to note that students using screen readers may have difficulty with frames. Typically, these applications read content in a linear fashion, reading one frame at a time. While the content of each frame is accessible, the relationship between the frames on the page may be difficult to understand. Adding a descriptive title to each `iframe` tag will help make them more accessible.

See also

▸ The *Embedding web videos and Creating audio files using Audacity* recipe in *Chapter 4, Working with Multimedia*

Using CSS to style content

By default, content created using the Learning Suite's HTML editor is un-styled. The `body` text uses a `serif` font on a white background and the spacing between the lines of text doesn't seem ideal for reading on a computer screen. The appearance of some items can be changed by selecting and formatting individual lines of text using the editor's toolbar. In this recipe, however, we'll look at a much better way to style our content in a way that looks cleaner and is easier to read.

We will be using **Cascading Style Sheets** (**CSS**) to define the presentation of the elements on our page. Using CSS, we are able to better separate the page's content from its visual appearance. This helps create web pages that are more accessible and also easier to maintain. We will start out by creating some embedded styles, which are styles defined in the HTML document itself. Then, we will learn how to move those styles to an external stylesheet, which can be referenced by many web pages at once. By using external stylesheets, you can easily change the appearance of all of your course's content at once.

The CSS we will be using is fairly basic; we're going to center the page's content and define some heading styles. After this recipe, you're welcome to continue adding to the stylesheet until you create something that you can use in all of your courses. If you're interested in using some great pre-built styles, the next recipe, *Using Desire2Learn's accessible templates*, would be a great place to start.

How to do it...

We're going to use some fairly simple CSS to adjust the look and feel of text in a content topic. Feel free to adjust any of the styles to match your own design preferences.

1. Access the **Content** area of your course.

2. Create a new **Topic** by clicking on the **Add Content** button and choosing the **New File** option. Go ahead and provide a title for the document and place it in an existing module. Click on the **Choose destination** button to select a location to save our file. Let's click on the **New Folder** button and create a folder named CSS. Select the new folder and click on the **Select a Path** button:

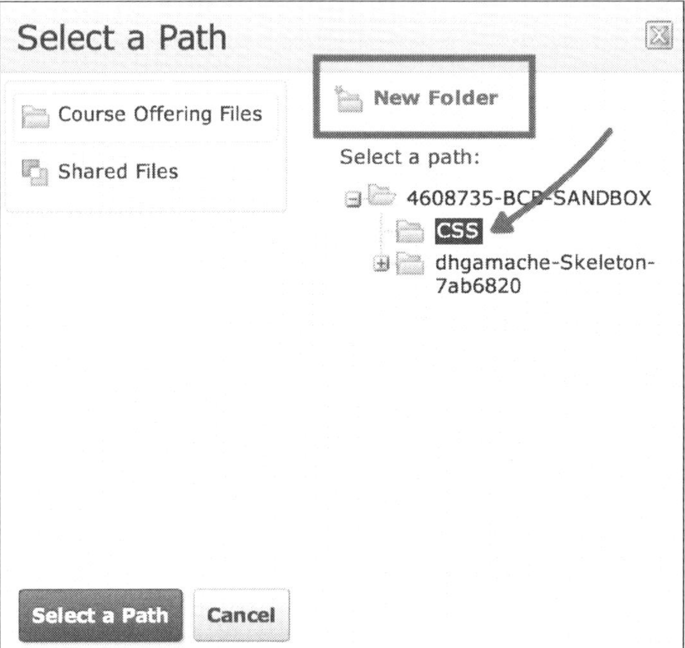

3. Position your cursor inside the HTML editor. Then, click on the small icon in the lower-left corner of the HTML editor to enter the source code view.

4. Place your cursor between the opening and closing <head> tags, and type the following code:

```css
<style type="text/css">
body {
margin: 0;
padding: 0;
border: 0;
background-color: #f2f2f2;
color: #3c3c3c;
font-size: 62.5%;
}

h1, h2 {
line-height:1.2em;
margin-top:32px;
margin-bottom:12px;
}

h3, h4, h5, h6 {
margin-top:12px;
margin-bottom:6px;
}

p {
margin:0 0 24px 0;
}

#content {
width: 650px;
margin: 0 auto 0 auto;
padding: 30px 0 30px 0;
font-family: 'Cochin', Palatino, Georgia, serif;
font-size: 1.7em;
line-height: 1.400000em;
}
</style>
```

5. Let's add some sample content for previewing our styles. Type the following code (feel free to substitute meaningful text for the placeholder text I'm using) between the opening and closing `<body>` tags:

```
<div id="wrapper">
<div id="content">
   <h1>Heading 1</h1>

   <p>Loremipsum dolor sitamet, consecteturadipiscingelit.
Fusce vitae est non puruseuismodpharetra.
Proinvelurnaveljustotinciduntpharetra.Curabiturodiotortor,
malesuada id sagittisnec, vehiculaquis.</p>

   <h2>Heading 2</h2>

   <p>Loremipsum dolor sitamet, consecteturadipiscingelit.
Fusce vitae est non puruseuismodpharetra.
Proinvelurnaveljustotinciduntpharetra.Curabiturodiotortor,
malesuada id sagittisnec, vehiculaquis.</p>

   <p>Loremipsum dolor sitamet, consecteturadipiscingelit.
Fusce vitae est non puruseuismodpharetra.
Proinvelurnaveljustotinciduntpharetra.Curabiturodiotortor,
malesuada id sagittisnec, vehiculaquis.</p>

</div><!-- End content -->
</div><!-- End wrapper -->
```

6. Click on the **Update** button. Then, save your work by clicking on the **Save** button.

7. Let's make sure everything worked as expected. Click on the **Preview** button at the top of the page to view the topic:

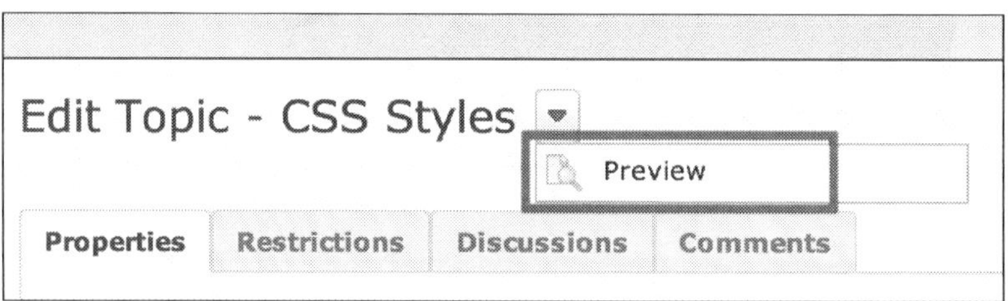

8. Your topic should look similar to the following screenshot:

Heading 1

Lorem ipsum dolor sit amet, consectetur adipiscing elit. Fusce vitae est non purus euismod pharetra. Proin vel urna vel justo tincidunt pharetra. Curabitur odio tortor, malesuada id sagittis nec, vehicula quis.

Heading 2

Lorem ipsum dolor sit amet, consectetur adipiscing elit. Fusce vitae est non purus euismod pharetra. Proin vel urna vel justo tincidunt pharetra. Curabitur odio tortor, malesuada id sagittis nec, vehicula quis.

Lorem ipsum dolor sit amet, consectetur adipiscing elit. Fusce vitae est non purus euismod pharetra. Proin vel urna vel justo tincidunt pharetra. Curabitur odio tortor, malesuada id sagittis nec, vehicula quis.

How it works...

Let's take a closer look at the CSS we typed in the page's <head> section. We start off by setting the margin, padding, and border or the page's <body> element to 0. Some browsers add default margins and padding to web pages, so resetting to 0 helps us create a more consistent experience between different browsers. We then set the background color of the page to a light gray color, assign a dark gray font color, and set the default font size. Feel free to experiment with different settings to create a look that works for you.

We then make some minimal changes to the heading tags, mostly adjusting their top and bottom margins. At the bottom of the style section, we create a selector for a `div` tag named `content`. This is where we will place all of the page's visible content. We set the width of the `content` div to `650` pixels and assign automatic left and right margins in order to center that element on the page. We finish up our style section by selecting a font family and setting a font size and line height. Again, feel free to experiment with different fonts and sizes until you find something that works for your course.

There's more...

So far, we've included all of our styles inside the HTML document. While this is acceptable, it doesn't harness the true power of CSS. Let's say we wanted to use the same styles in another content topic. We would need to copy all the code we just typed into the new document. In addition, if we later decide to adjust one or more of the styles, we would need to manually edit each document.

Fortunately, there's an easy way to fix this problem. We can move all of the CSS into an external stylesheet and then reference that sheet in each of our documents using a single line of code. Even better, since each document is linked to a centralized stylesheet, we only need to update one file to change the look and feel of many documents. Let's see how it works!

1. Access your course and navigate to the **Content** tool.

2. Locate the document we created earlier in this recipe and select the **Edit** option from the context menu:

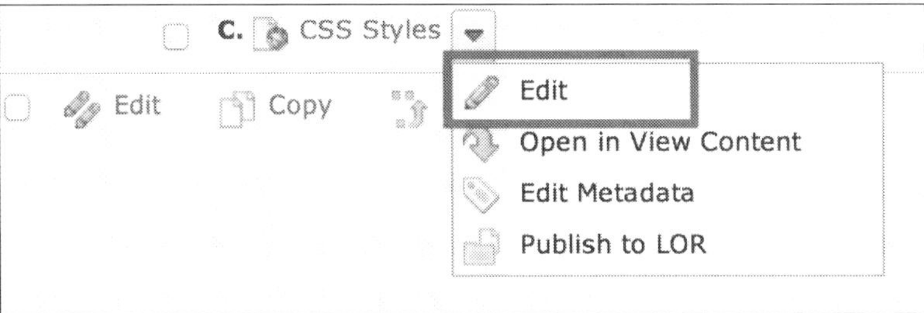

3. Access the source code editor by clicking on the small icon in the bottom-left corner of the HTML editor.

4. Select all of the styles between the opening and closing `<style>` tags.

5. Using a text editor (or HTML editor if you have one), create a new plain text file and paste all of the code we just copied into the document.

6. Save the document on your desktop with the name `styles.css`:

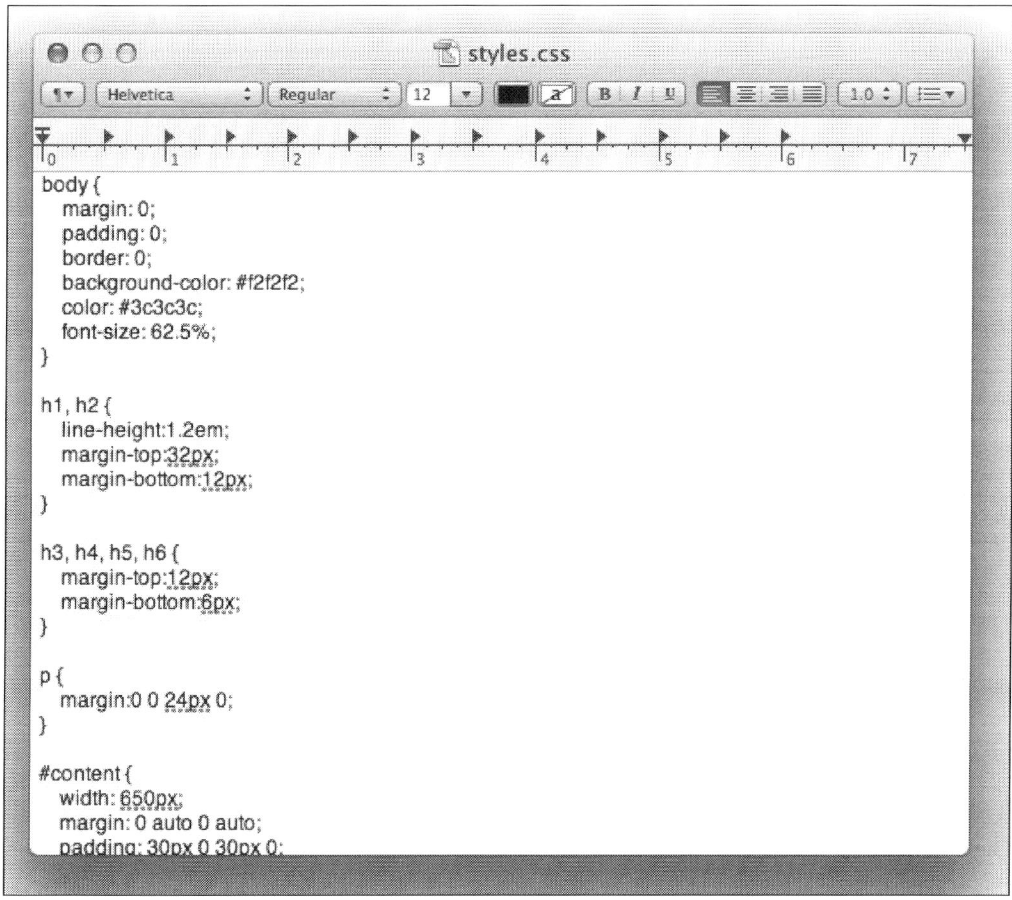


```css
body {
    margin: 0;
    padding: 0;
    border: 0;
    background-color: #f2f2f2;
    color: #3c3c3c;
    font-size: 62.5%;
}

h1, h2 {
    line-height:1.2em;
    margin-top:32px;
    margin-bottom:12px;
}

h3, h4, h5, h6 {
    margin-top:12px;
    margin-bottom:6px;
}

p {
    margin:0 0 24px 0;
}

#content {
    width: 650px;
    margin: 0 auto 0 auto;
    padding: 30px 0 30px 0;
```

7. Return to the HTML editor in your online course and delete all of the styles we just copied. Make sure to delete the opening `<style>` and closing `</style>` tag as well.

8. Add the following line of code in your document's `<head>` tag:

```
<linkrel="stylesheet" href="styles.css" title="Main Style Sheet"
type="text/css" media="screen" charset="utf-8">
```

9. Click on **Update**, then press the **Save** button to save changes to the web page. Notice that our nice formatting has disappeared. Don't worry, we will take care of that momentarily.

10. Access the **File Manager** for your course by clicking on the **Manage Files** tab at the top of the page in the **Content** tool. Select the CSS folder in the left column, then click on the **Upload** icon at the top of the center column:

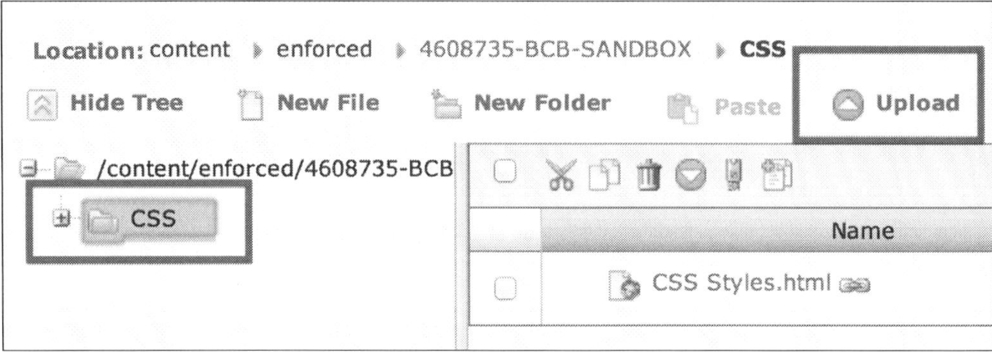

11. Select the CSS file we saved to the desktop. Then click on the **Upload** button.

12. Try previewing our original content item again. You should see the styles applied once again.

13. To use the stylesheet with any new documents, just take the code from step 8, paste it in the new page's header, and you're all set!

See also

▸   The *Displaying external web content with frames and Using Desire2Learn's accessible templates* recipes

Using Desire2Learn's accessible templates

Desire2Learn's accessible templates are collections of HTML files and CSS that make it relatively easy for you to dramatically change the look of your course documents, while making the content more accessible to your students. In this recipe, we'll learn how to create our own content using these templates.

Getting ready

Desire2Learn currently offers four accessible templates for download at `http://www.desire2learn.com/products/accessibility/instructor-resources/HTML-templates/`. Go ahead and choose the template that you would like to use; I am going to use the **Ordinary Blue** template in the steps below. You can easily change templates later, so don't feel like you're stuck with your initial choice.

Click on either the template name or the image to download the necessary files. Pay attention to where the `.zip` file is saved—we'll need to locate it shortly. We'll also be adding an image to our document, so you will need to have an appropriately sized image saved somewhere on your computer.

How to do it...

We're going to learn how to upload the templates and integrate them within the content tool of a Desire2Learn Learning Suite course. We will not cover all of the styles and features available in the templates, but you can reference the included theme documentation for more details after we complete the initial setup.

1. Access the Desire2Learn Learning Suite course in which you'd like to use the templates.

2. Let's head over to the **File Manager**. Click on the **Edit Course** link in the course navigation bar. Then, click on the **Manage Files** link.

3. Click on the **Upload** button at the top of the center column. Click on the **Choose File** button and locate the `.zip` folder containing the template files. Select the file and click on **Open**.

4. Click on the **Upload** button.

5. Once the upload is complete, you'll see it added to your file list. Hover over the title until the contex menu appears, then click on the **unzip** icon:

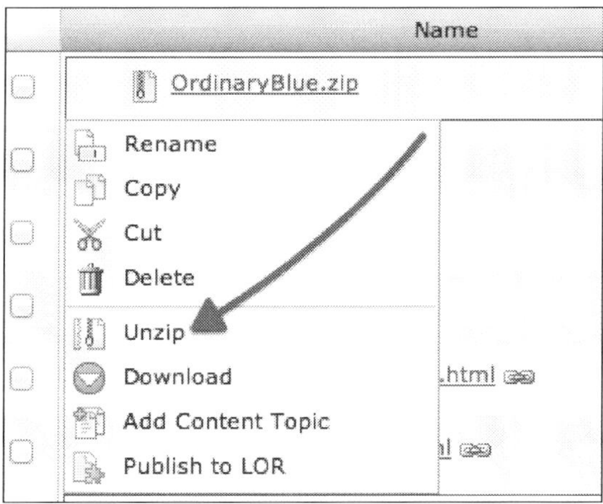

6. Once the file has been unzipped, select the original `.zip` folder and delete it; we no longer need that file.

7. Access the template's folder by clicking on its title. Hover over **HowToUseThisTemplate.html** until the context menu appears. Choose the **Copy** option:

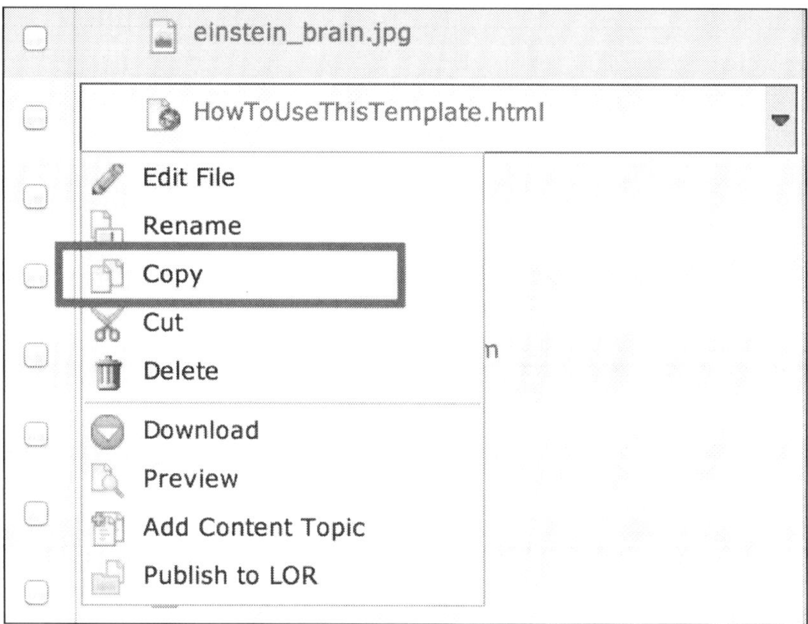

8. Now, click on the **Paste** button in the header to paste our copy back into the file list. Let's activate the context menu for the newly copied file and choose the **Rename** option.

9. Enter a new name for the document and click on the **Save** button.

10. Create a content topic for our new document by hovering over the title again and choosing the **Add Content Topic** link. When prompted, choose a module, provide a title, and click on the **Save** button.

11. Navigate to the **Content** tool and click on the **edit** (pencil) icon to the right of your new topic. Go ahead and select the **Heading** text at the top. The styles drop-down list changes to show you that the format of the selected text is **Heading 1**. Change the Heading to something appropriate for your course:

12. Highlight all of the content between the heading and the footer. Once selected, type a sentence or two of text. Make sure to highlight your text once you are finished and assign the **Paragraph** formatting to it using the **Styles** drop-down menu.

13. Let's go ahead and add a sub-heading to our document. Press the *Return* or *Enter* key to move the cursor to a new line. Then, type the text for your new line. Once finished, go ahead and select the entire line and apply the **Heading 2** formatting to it.

14. Type another paragraph, making sure it is assigned the **Paragraph** style from the drop-down list. While you're at it, highlight the placeholder text in the footer and replace it with something more appropriate for your course.

15. Let's add an image to our document. Click on the image icon in the editor's toolbar. Then, click on the **Choose File** button, select an image file from your computer, and click on **Open**. Click on the **Upload** button. Make sure to provide some alternative text for the image when prompted.

16. We need to do some work in the source code view now, so go ahead and click on the icon in the lower-left corner of the editor window. Locate the image's `<img>` tag. Position your cursor before the tag and type `<div class="imgRight">`. Then, position your cursor after the closing `</img>` tag, and type `</div>`.

```
<p>
<div class="imgRight">
<img src="/content/enforced/3839437-B
</div>
</p>
```

17. While still in the HTML source view, locate the second paragraph that we typed into the WYSIWYG interface. Look for the opening paragraph tag and change it to `<p class="note">`.

18. Click on the **Update** button.

19. Press the **Save** button, then check out your work using the **Preview** option in context menu at the top of the page.

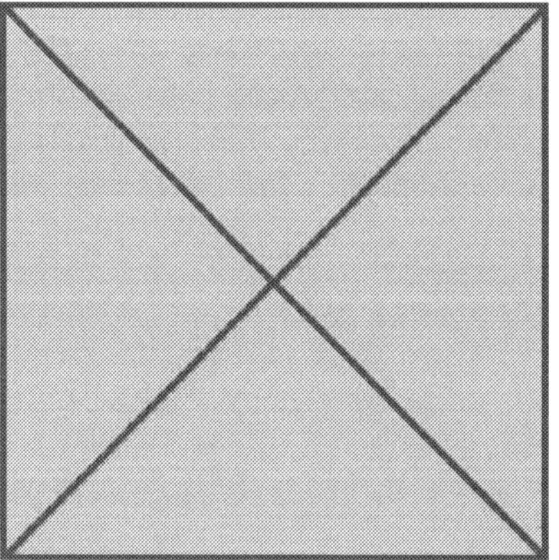

How it works...

We start this recipe by uploading the theme's `.zip` folder to the file manager of a Desire2Learn Learning Suite course. If you extract the folder, you'll see that each theme contains a folder named `TemplateFiles` that contains the CSS and images to give the theme its unique appearance. You can switch to another theme at any point by simply replacing this folder with the same folder from another theme.

After extracting the folder, we duplicate **HowToUseThisTheme.html**. This file contains detailed instructions and example code for using the theme, so we definitely don't want to override the original. After completing this recipe, I recommend reading this page thoroughly to learn about all of the theme's capabilities. We use the **Add Content Topic** option in the context menu to create a new topic for the uploaded file. This allows us to access the file from within the **Content** tool. Students are not able to browse files in the file manager, so make sure to create a topic for each document you want students to be able to view.

In step 16, we wrap our `<img>` tag with a `div` tag of the `imgRight` class. This floats the enclosed image to the right side of the page. In case you're wondering, there's also an `imgLeft` class that you could use to float the image to the left side of the page. We also assign the "note" style to one of the paragraphs in the document.

I frequently find myself adding text using the HTML editor's WYSIWYG interface, returning to source code view when I need to assign special styles to images and text. If you work the same way and are editing larger documents, then locating the code you want to alter can be time-consuming. However, if you copy a few words of the paragraph from the WYSIWYG interface, you can use the browser's built-in search functionality, available using the keyboard shortcut *Ctrl/Cmd + F*, to locate the text in the source code view.

See also

- The *Using CSS to style content* recipe
- The *Using your profile to add personality* recipe in *Chapter 2, Personalizing Your Course*

Creating mobile-friendly content

Mobile device usage has skyrocketed over the past few years. As a result, it has become increasingly important to create course materials that look great and function on a variety of screen sizes. You're probably aware that Desire2Learn Learning Suite offers a mobile-optimized version of the LMS that can be accessed by logging into the system from a recognized mobile device. The techniques detailed in this recipe will work irrespective of whether students access the material using that interface or the standard desktop interface. In fact, the code contained in this recipe will even solve some common problems with the mobile web view!

How to do it...

In this recipe, we will look at a couple of simple techniques for making your course content look great on screen sizes ranging from smartphones to tablets and desktop computers.

1. Access your course and navigate to the **Content** tool.

2. Create a new topic and choose the **New File** option.

3. Provide a title in the text field and select an existing module in which our document is to be placed.

4. We need some content to work with, so take a few minutes to type in a few paragraphs of text, upload an image or two, and embed a YouTube video. Please see the *Embedding Web Videos* recipe in *Chapter 4* for more information on adding videos from YouTube, Vimeo, or other video hosting sites.

5. Click on the small icon in the lower-left corner of the editor to edit the HTML source code.

6. Position your cursor inside the page's opening and closing `<head>` tags, and type the following code:

```
<meta name="viewport" content="width=device-width, initial-scale=1">
```

7. Let's add a bit of CSS just before the closing `</head>` tag:

```
<style type="text/css">

img, iframe {
        max-width: 100%;
}

</style>
```

8. Click on the Update button to return to exit the source view. Then, save your work by clicking the **Save** button.

How it works...

The few lines of code we added in the HTML source view has made a big impact on the page's appearance. Without these changes, our page would have looked similar to the following screenshot when viewed on a mobile device:

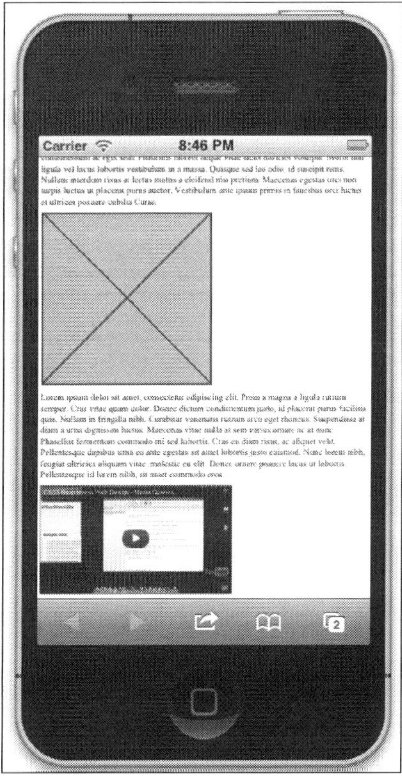

Notice how small the text is on the screen. Mobile browsers render web pages in a virtual window (viewport) that's typically wider than the device's actual screen. Mobile Safari, for example, uses a default viewport of **980** pixels. This helps shrink a desktop site down to fit on the smaller screen and minimizes horizontal scrolling. However, it also makes the text difficult to read. The line of code we added to the header sets the viewport to be equal to the width of the device's screen, which means our users won't have to zoom and pan to view the content.

We experience a different, but equally annoying, problem if we view the page using Desire2Learn Learning Suite's mobile web interface. Because both the image and the video are wider than the device's viewport, they disappear off the sides of the page. Students accessing the page on a mobile device would still have to scroll the page or zoom out in order to see our media:

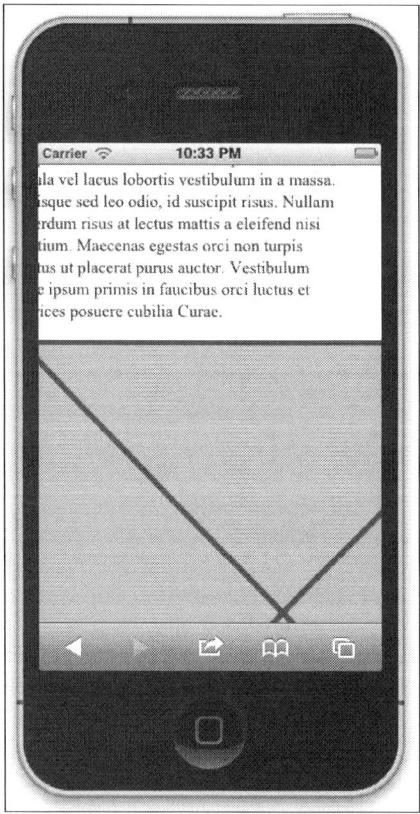

We fix this problem by adding some CSS to the page header. We simply set the maximum width of the image and iFrame (YouTube videos are embedded in iFrames) elements to be 100 percent. This means that the item can be no larger than the element in which it is contained. Since we set the viewport to be equal to the device width, the image will automatically shrink to fit the window in which it is presented. You can test this on your desktop by opening the page and resizing the browser window. As the window gets smaller, the image and video should resize accordingly!

See also

> ▶ The *Displaying external web content with frames, Using CSS to style content,* and *Using Desire2Learn's accessible templates* recipes

6
Managing Assessments

In this chapter, we will cover the following recipes:

- Streamlining the quiz creation process using quiz templates
- Copying quiz questions to the question library
- Giving students extra time on assessments
- Deleting a student's quiz attempt
- Using question feedback to help students learn
- Using submission views and release conditions to create a learning experience
- Submitting a quiz on behalf of a student
- Minimizing cheating by randomizing questions and options
- Correcting quiz questions

Introduction

The recipes in this chapter are all focused on using and managing assessments effectively. We start by discussing ways of speeding up the quiz creation process by creating quiz templates and publishing questions to the question library. Next, we discuss how to give individual students extra time on assessments. In later recipes, we'll use question feedback and multiple submission views to transform assessments into learning activities. We wrap up the chapter by discussing how to minimize cheating by randomizing both questions and question options.

Streamlining the quiz creation process using quiz templates

The Desire2Learn Learning Suite offers instructors quite a bit of flexibility in how quizzes are created and administered. Among other options, you determine when a quiz is available, how much time a student is given to complete an assessment, and even what information is displayed to students after an attempt has been submitted. Because you're responsible for configuring all of these options when you create a new quiz, starting from scratch can be a time-consuming process. For assessments with similar settings, such as weekly homework quizzes, it may be easier to create an assessment from a template instead of starting from the beginning each time. In this recipe, we'll create a template and discuss how to copy it to create future assessments.

Getting ready

In the following steps, I refer to assessments as **Quizzes**. Your institution may use a different name, such as **Exams**, so you may need to adjust the steps accordingly.

How to do it...

In this recipe, we'll walk through the steps to create an example of a weekly homework quiz. Once we configure the quiz's basic properties, attempts, and submission views, we will use it as a template to create another, similar assessment.

1. Access your course and navigate to the **Quizzes** tool.

2. Click on the **New Quiz** button to create a new, empty quiz.

3. Type `Homework Quiz Template` in the **Name** field. Then, click on the **Add Category** link.

4. Type **Homework Quizzes** in the **Name** field, and click on the **Save** button.

5. Visit the **Restrictions** tab and set a time limit of 15 minutes. Check the **enforced** option.

6. Access the **Submission Views** tab and click on the **Default View** link. Choose the **Show questions answered incorrectly** option. Then, click on the **Save View** button:

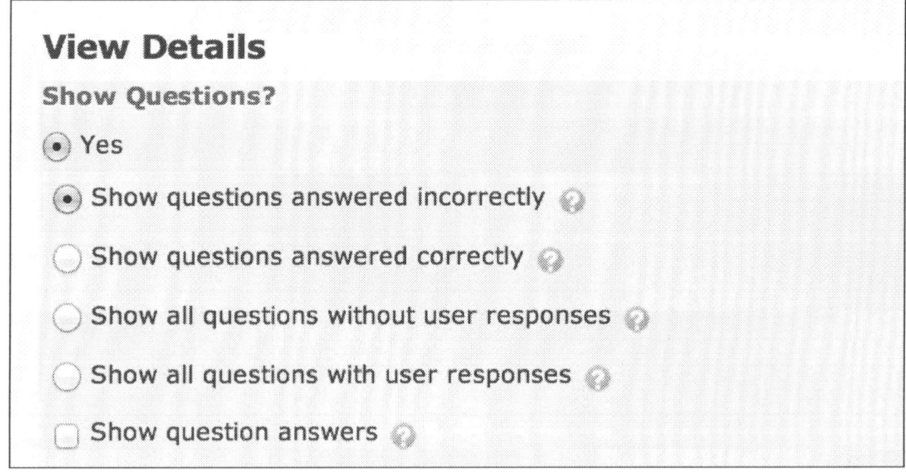

7. We now have our quiz template set up and ready to use. Let's create a new **Homework** quiz by navigating back to the list of quizzes. Click on the **Copy** button.

8. Choose the **Homework Quiz Template** in the **Quiz to Copy** drop-down list.

9. Change the default name to `Week 1 Homework Quiz`.

10. Leave the status as inactive, check the **Edit Quiz after copy completes** option, and click on **Save**:

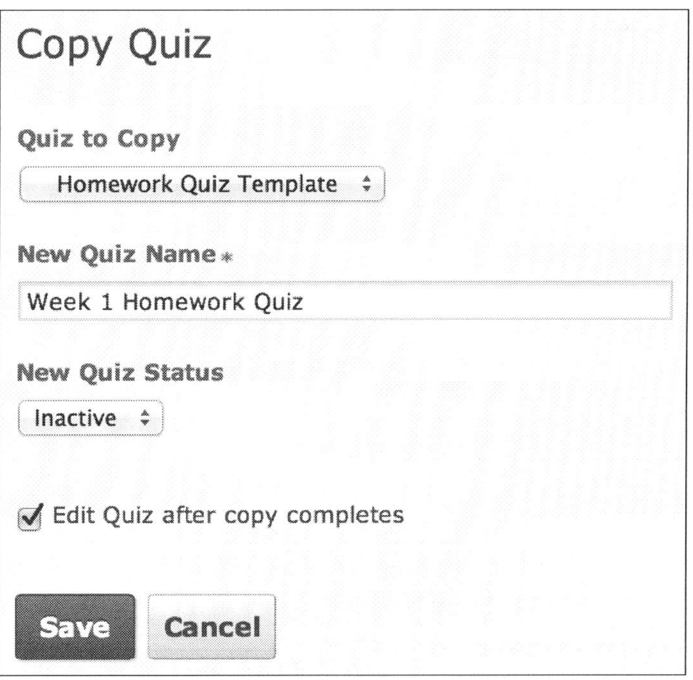

How it works...

We start this recipe by creating a new quiz that will become our template. Since we plan on using this quiz template to create all of our weekly homework quizzes, we assigned to the **Homework Quizzes** category. We also set a time limit and **Modified Default Submission View** to show students the questions they answered incorrectly. Of course, you should adjust the steps in this recipe to match the requirements for your own quizzes. The important thing to remember is that you want to go ahead and define any settings that will be the same in all future quizzes created using this template. Make sure that you leave the quiz set to **Inactive** on the **Restrictions** tab. You don't want students to have access to the template.

Once the template is complete, you can create a new quiz at any time by choosing the **Copy** option, just as we did in steps 7 to 10. New quizzes created by copying this template will retain all of the settings of the original. You can modify any settings that differ once the quiz has been created. You'll also need to add questions to the assessment and set the start and end dates before giving the students' access. Remember to change the status to **Active**, and click on the **Save** button when you're done.

See also

> ▸ The *Copying quiz questions to the question library* recipe

Copying quiz questions to the question library

Assessment questions can be created either in the **Layout/Questions** section of an individual quiz or in your course's **Question Library**, a centralized database of questions that can be referenced from any assessment in your course. If you plan on using a question in multiple quizzes or exams, such as a unit test and final exams, then it makes sense to move questions to the question library. Doing so frees you from the time-consuming process of retyping each question in multiple exams and also makes editing questions easier; you can modify a question in one location and update all of its occurrences in your course.

Getting ready

We're not going to be creating any questions in this recipe, so you'll need to have an existing quiz containing at least a few questions.

How to do it...

In this recipe, we'll learn how to copy questions from an existing quiz to the question library.

1. Access your course and navigate to the **Quizzes** tool.

2. Click on the link to access **Question Library**.

3. Click on the **New** button and select the **Section** option in the **Create New** drop-down list.

4. Provide a name for the new section. Then, click on **Save**.

5. Click on the title of the newly created section in the list of **Question Library** items.

6. Click on the **Import** button.

7. Select **From an Existing Collection** in the **Import Source** drop-down list. Choose the quiz from which you want to copy questions in the **Source Collection** drop-down list. Choose **Collection Root** for **Source Collection**.

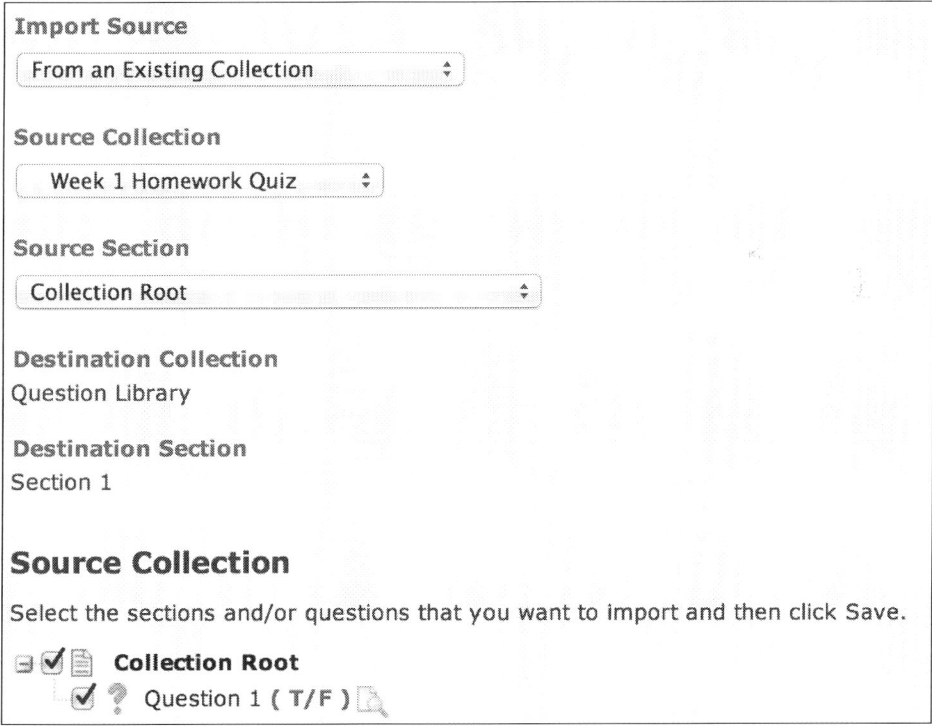

8. Select the top checkbox (Collection Root) to import all questions in the selected assessment. Then, Click on the **Save** button.

How it works...

Sections in **Question Library** are similar to folders on your PC—they're used to store groups of related items. You can organize your question library however you'd like, but I recommend creating a new section for each assessment in your course. Once you've created a section, you can import either individual quiz questions or entire collections from existing quizzes. In this recipe, we imported everything by selecting the **Collection Root** checkbox.

There's more...

There will probably be times when you need to modify a question after it has been created. By using the question library you only have to edit the question in one location to modify all of its occurrences in a course. Let's say, for example, you have used the same question in a weekly quiz and the final exam. Rather than visiting each quiz to modify the question, we simply edit the question in one location and select the checkboxes to update all occurrences of the question throughout the course:

> ### Question In Use
>
> This question is used in more than one place.
> Select all the items you want the changes to apply to then click the **Save** button.
>
> ☐
>
> **Question Library**
> ☑ Question Library
> **Quizzes**
> ☑ Week 1 Homework Quiz
> ☑ Final Exam
>
> ☐

Importing questions from the question library

So far, we've only discussed about importing questions into the question library. However, the library isn't too useful unless you're also able to pull questions from it into new quizzes. The following steps describe that process:

1. Access a quiz and navigate to the **Layout/Questions** tab.

2. Click on the **Add/Edit Questions** button and click on the **Import** button.

3. Choose the **From an Existing Collection in the Import Source** drop-down list:

Import Source

From an Existing Collection

Source Collection

Question Library

Source Section

Unit 1 Questions

Destination Collection
Final Exam

Destination Section
Final Exam (root)

Source Collection

Select the sections and/or questions that you want to import and then click Save.

☑ 📁 Unit 1 Questions
 ☑ ❔ Question 1 (T/F)

4. Select **Question Library** for **Source Collection**.

5. Choose the appropriate section in the **Source Section** drop-down list.

6. Select the checkboxes next to the question you want to import into the quiz or choose the top checkbox to import all of the questions in the section.

7. Click on **Save**.

See also

> ▸ The *Copying course materials from a previous semester* recipe in *Chapter 1, Getting Your Course Ready for a New Semester*

Giving students extra time on assessments

The **Restrictions** tab in the **Quizzes** tool allows you to set the availability and time limit of a quiz for all students in your course. However, you may need to give individual students, such as those with disabilities, additional time to complete an assignment. Or, you may need to make an exam available during a different time period for students who are unable to take an exam during the designated timeframe.

Getting ready

You'll need an existing quiz in order to complete this recipe. If you don't already have one available, go ahead and create one now. Make sure you've defined a start and end date along with a time limit for the quiz.

How to do it...

In this recipe, we'll use the **Advanced Availability** settings to overwrite the universal availability dates and time period for an assessment.

1. Access a quiz and click on the **Restrictions** tab.

2. Verify that the availability dates and timings are correct.

3. In the **Advanced Availability** section, make sure that the **Allow selected users special access to this quiz** radio button is selected:

Advanced Availability

Advanced Availability

(●) Allow selected users special access to this quiz

( ) Allow only users with special access to see this quiz

Add Users to Special Access

4. Click on the **Add Users to Special Access** button.

5. Assign a special start or end date in the section at the top of the page or select a special time limit in the **Access** section.

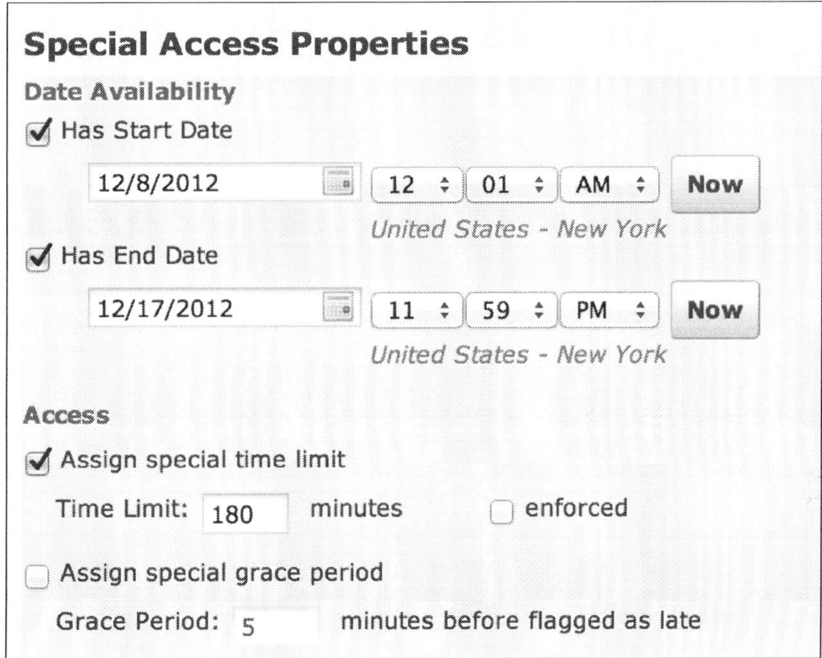

6. Under the **Users** heading at the bottom of the page, select the checkbox next to each student to whom you want to assign special access:

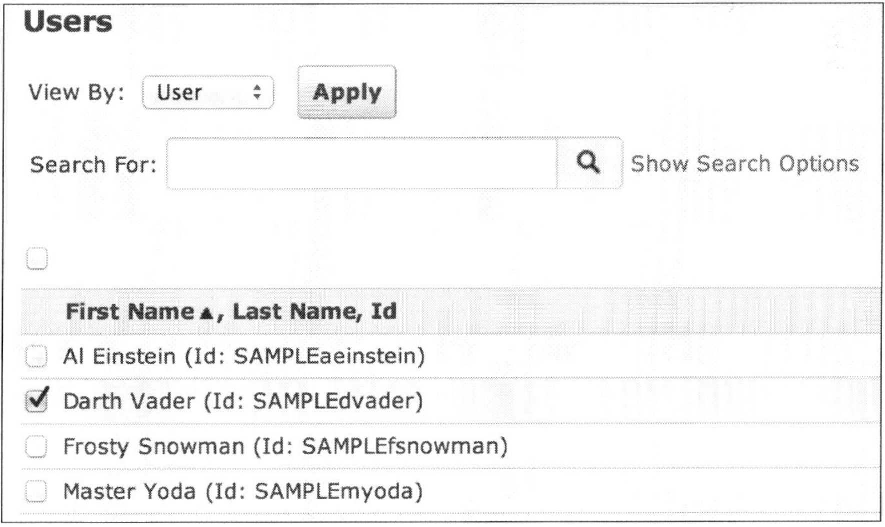

7. Click on the **Add Special Access** button.

8. Click on the **Save Quiz** button.

How it works...

Use the **Advanced Availability** section of the **Restrictions** tab to assign different quiz availability dates, time limits, or late submission options to specific users. Choose the **Allow selected users special access to this quiz** option when you want to override the quiz's regular restrictions for a small number of students. For example, you would use this option to give a student additional time to complete a quiz or allow someone to take their quiz before or after the regular availability dates. You'd choose the **Allow only users with special access to see this quiz** option when you want to make an assessment available to only a selected number of students. This option is useful for make-up exams.

After you click on the **Add Users to Special Access** button, select the **Special Access** properties at the top of the page. The options you select here override the general restrictions for the quiz, so you only need to modify the settings that will be different from the overall restrictions. For example, when creating special access for a student who only needs additional time to complete an exam, there's no need to specify a start and end date on the **Special Access Properties** screen. Select the checkboxes next to each student's name that will receive special access. After clicking on the **Add Special Access** button, you can repeat the same process to add multiple levels of special access for different students. It's important to note that you will need to save the quiz after adding advanced availability for students. If you navigate away from the quiz before saving, you'll lose your work.

Once a student has been given special access to an assessment, you'll see the student's name at the bottom of the **Advanced Availability** section. You can edit the availability or remove it altogether using the pencil or trashcan icons next to the student's name:

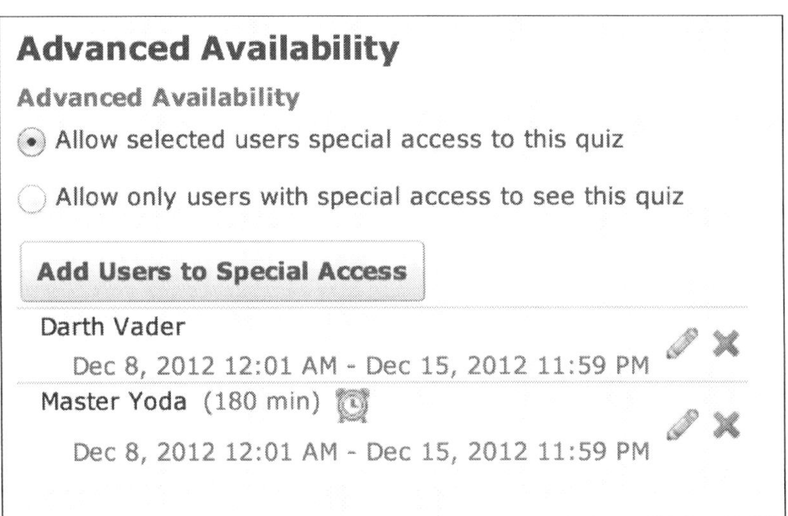

Deleting a student's quiz attempt

Sometimes students experience technical difficulties that prevent them from completing an assessment. This can be due to system downtime, loss of Internet access, and even hardware failure. Other times, you may just want to give students another shot at a particularly difficult exam. In either case, you'll need to delete the current attempt in order to allow them to start again.

Getting ready

The following steps detail the process for searching and deleting assessment attempts. Since it's not possible to restore a deleted attempt, you'll want to follow these steps only when you have an actual student attempt you need to delete.

How to do it...

In this recipe, we'll learn how to manually delete an on-going or previously submitted attempt.

1. Access your course and navigate to the **Quizzes** tool.

2. Access the context menu for the quiz and click on the **Grade** option (ruler and checkmark).

3. Click on the **Display Options** button and make sure the **Allow Reset** option is checked:

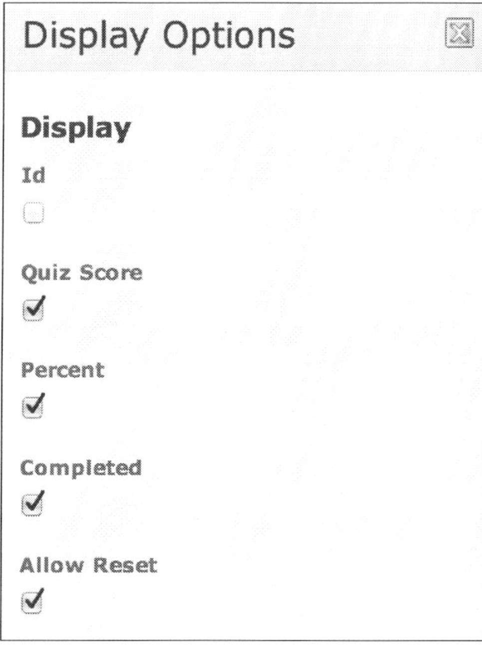

4. Click on **Save**.

5. Locate the attempt you'd like to delete.

6. Check the box next to the attempt and click on the trashcan icon:

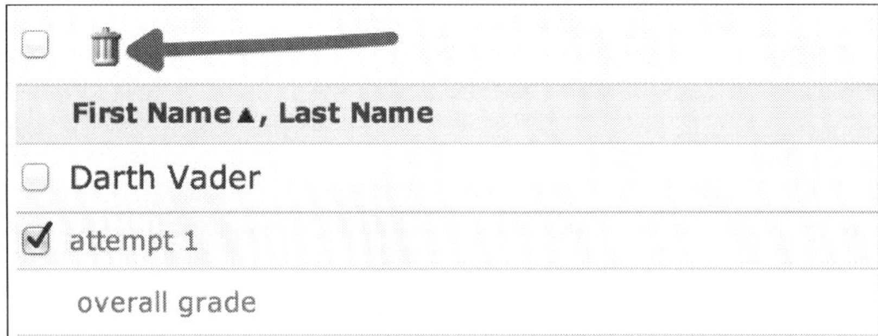

7. When prompted, click on the **Yes** button to permanently delete the attempt.

How it works...

The most important part of the process is enabling the **Allow Reset** option. Once enabled, you'll see checkboxes next to each attempt in either the **Users** or **Attempts** tabs. The system will remember your settings, so you won't need to click on the **Display Options** button each time you need to delete an attempt. By default, you will only see attempts that have been completed and submitted. If you need to delete an attempt that is in progress, or never submitted, make sure to change the **Restrict to** drop-down option to **Users with attempts in progress**. You'll need to click on the magnifying glass icon to filter the results after making the change.

Using question feedback to help students learn

You probably leave comments on traditional, paper-based exams when you return them to students. Doing so helps students understand why they missed particular questions and also helps them learn from their mistakes. The Desire2Learn Learning Environment offers several ways to leave helpful comments on electronic submissions. You can use the system's feedback options to explain difficult questions, link to additional information in online resources, and more. You can even combine feedback with submission options to create learning experiences from your assessments.

Getting ready

You'll need a quiz with at least one question to complete this recipe. I'll be working with a multiple choice question, but the following steps will be similar for other types as well. While experimenting with the different options available, I recommend using a quiz that is currently inactive. In order to leave an attempt feedback, you'll need access to a quiz with at least one student submission.

How to do it...

In this recipe, we'll learn how to leave feedback on questions, individual question options, and even for the whole attempt.

1. Access your course and navigate to the **Quizzes** tool.

2. Click on the title of the quiz that contains the question for which you want to leave a feedback.

3. Access the **Layout/Questions** tab and click on the **Add/Edit Questions** button.

4. Activate the context menu for a question and choose the **Edit** (pencil) icon.

5. Locate the feedback box for the first option. Position your cursor inside the textbox and type a comment that will be seen by students that select that particular option.

6. Repeat the same process for each question option.

7. Locate the **Question Feedback** section at the bottom of the page. You may need to click on the **Expand question feedback** link in order to see it.

8. Position your cursor in the textbox and type a comment that will be shown to everyone, regardless of the of the option they select.

9. Click on **Save**.

10. Now that we've left comments on a question, we need to enable feedback for the quiz. Go ahead and access the **Submission Views** tab and click on the **Default view** link.

11. Select the options to show questions. Then, select the **Show all questions with user responses** option:

View Details

Show Questions?

- ⦿ Yes
  - ○ Show questions answered incorrectly ❓
  - ○ Show questions answered correctly ❓
  - ○ Show all questions without user responses ❓
  - ⦿ Show all questions with user responses ❓
  - ☐ Show question answers ❓
  - ☑ Show question score and out of score
- ○ No ❓

12. Click on the **Save** button.

How it works...

You can provide feedback in two different places. Feedback left for a particular option is only shown if a student selects that option. For incorrect options, you may want to provide some information that explains why another choice is better, link to pertinent items in the course content, or refer back to the course's learning objectives. Any comments left in the **Question Feedback** area are shown no matter what option the student selects. This is a good place to provide general feedback.

In order for students to view the feedback we just typed, you'll need to activate the option to show questions in the **Submission Views** tab. In this recipe, we chose the option to show all the questions, but you may want to only show the questions answered correctly or those that were answered incorrectly.

There's more...

So far, we've left feedback that will be automatically presented to students based on the preferences we've defined. However, you may also want to leave comments for individual students. We can do that when grading an attempt.

1. From the **Manage Quizzes** page, activate the context menu for the quiz and select the **Grade** option (ruler and checkmark).

2. Click on a student's attempt.

3. Type some feedback for the attempt in the textbox under the **Grading Feedback** heading:

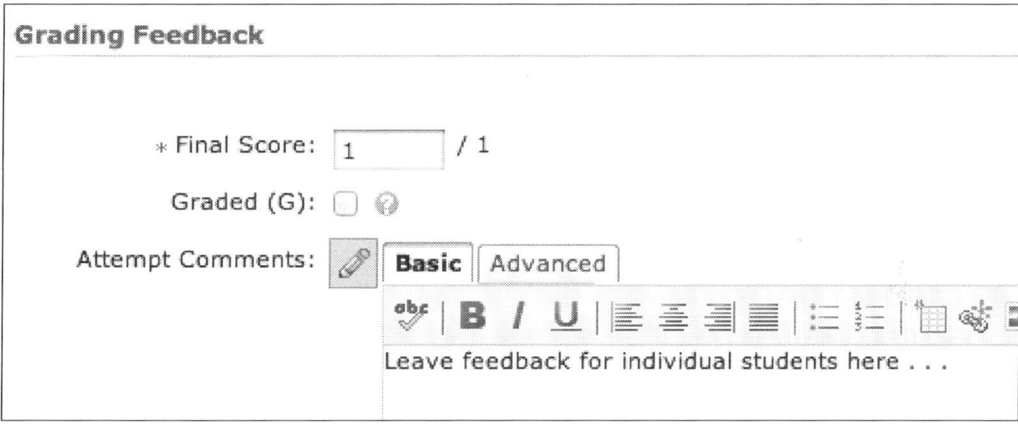

4. Click on **Save** when finished.

See also

- The *Using submission views and release conditions to create a learning experience* recipe

Using submission views and release conditions to create a learning experience

In online courses, it's often more difficult to determine when students understand concepts than in the traditional classroom environment. In order to measure comprehension and make sure students have a solid foundation before moving on to more advanced topics, we'll introduce a non-graded "self-check" quiz in this recipe. We'll give the students an unlimited number of attempts on the assessment and restrict access to the unit exam until they have mastered the background material. While this may sound difficult to accomplish, the Learning Environment's tools make it an easy task. This recipe is just one example of what's possible by combining multiple tools to solve problems.

Getting ready

Before beginning the following steps, take a few minutes to create both a self-check quiz and a graded test.

How to do it...

In the following steps, we'll use multiple attempts, submission views, and release conditions to help students better prepare for an online test. After learning the basics here, you can modify these steps to better fir your own course.

1. Access your course and navigate to the **Quizzes** tool.

2. Click on the title of the self-check quiz to adjust its settings.

3. Access the **Attempts** tab and select the **Unlimited** option in the **Attempts Allowed** drop-down list.

4. Click on the **Save Quiz** button.

5. Let's navigate to the **Submission Views** tab and make a quick change there as well. Make sure that **Default View** is set to not show questions:

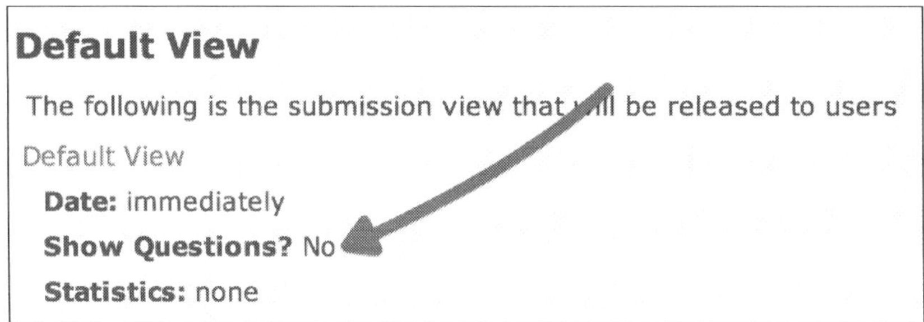

6. Click on the **Add Additional View** button and provide a name for our new view.

7. Under the **View Restrictions** heading, choose a date several days after students need to successfully complete the assessment. Choose the **Show all questions with user responses** and **Show questions answers** options:

View Details

Show Questions?

- ◉ Yes
  - ○ Show questions answered incorrectly
  - ○ Show questions answered correctly
  - ○ Show all questions without user responses
  - ◉ Show all questions with user responses
  - ☑ Show question answers
  - ☑ Show question score and out of score
- ○ No

8. Click on the **Save** button.

9. Now, let's access the module test by returning to the quiz list and clicking on the title of the examination.

10. Access the **Restrictions** tab. Click on the **Create and Attach** button in the **Release Conditions** section.

11. Choose **Score on a Quiz** in the **Condition Type** drop-down list.

12. Select the name of the self-check quiz in the **Quiz** menu.

13. Change the criteria to **<=** and type 80 in the **Grade** text field. The number you type here determines the minimum score on the practice test required to take the graded exam. So, feel free to change it to the one that better matches your course objectives.

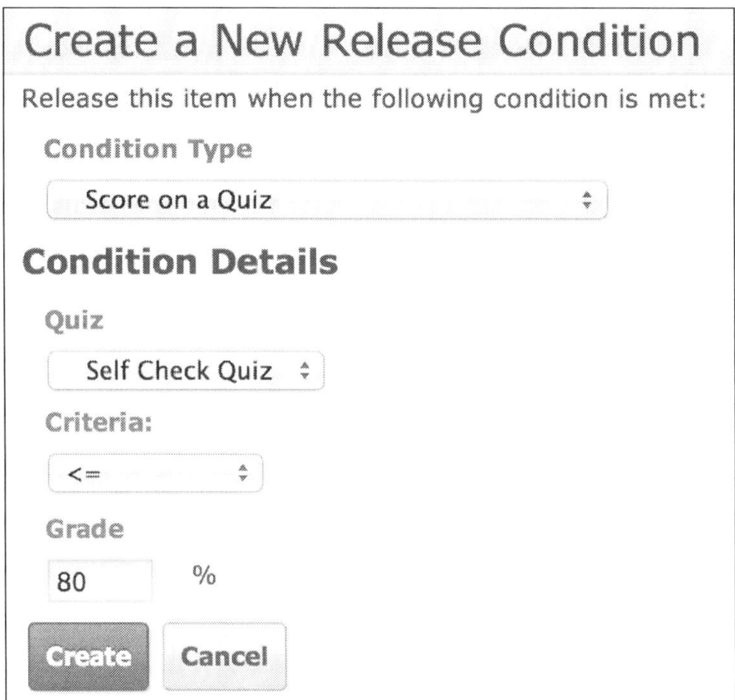

14. Click on the **Create** button. Then, click on the **Save** button.

How it works...

Our goal in this recipe is to create a self-check quiz that helps students measure their own understanding of the topic and also prevents them from attempting the unit exam until they earn an acceptable score, in our case 80 percent, on our practice quiz. We began by allowing an unlimited number of attempts on the self-check quiz, so that students can continue taking the exam until they have mastered the material. Since it wouldn't be too useful to show students the correct answers until they earn a passing score on the assessment, we set a future date to show the answers and question feedback to the students.

Next, we applied a release condition to the module test that requires the students earn a score of at least 80 percent in order to be able to access it. If you're using the Grades tool in your course, you can also associate the module test with a grade item to automatically record the students' scores.

See also

> ▸ The *Streamlining the quiz creation process using quiz templates, Using question feedback to help students learn,* and *Minimizing cheating by randomizing questions and options* recipes

Submitting a quiz on behalf of a student

Sometimes students experience technical difficulties that prevent them from submitting an assessment. Other times, they may close their browsers before completing the submission process or simply forget to submit their work after saving all of their answers. In either case, you're not able to grade their work until the attempt has been successfully submitted. Fortunately, the system allows us to enter an on-going quiz and submit it on behalf of the student.

Getting ready

We're going to be submitting an attempt in-progress. So you'll need both an active quiz and an on-going attempt in order to complete this recipe.

How to do it...

1. Access your course and navigate to the **Quizzes** tool.

2. Activate the context menu for the quiz and select the **Grade** option.

3. In the **Users** tab, change the **Restrict to** drop-down list to **Users with attempts in progress**, and click on the **Search** button.

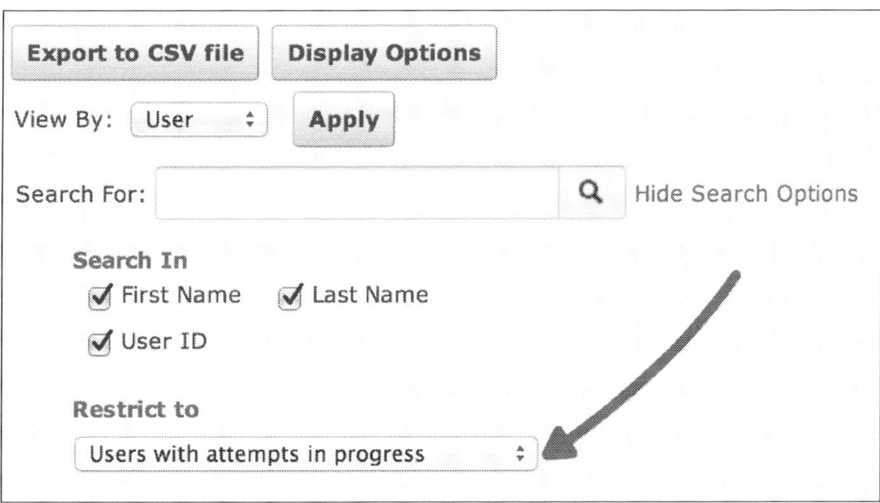

4. Click on the **Enter Quiz as User** icon to the right of an attempt to enter the quiz as that student:

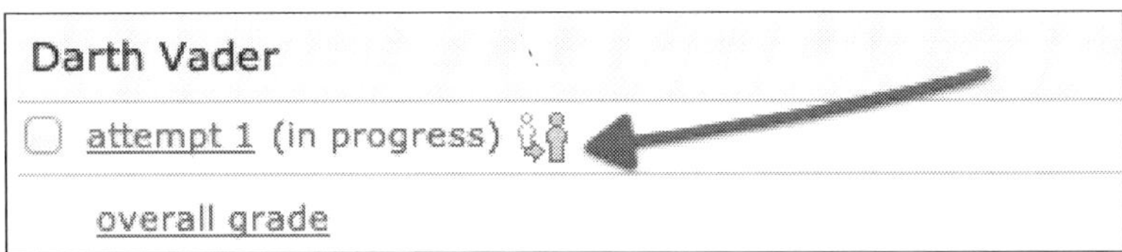

5. When prompted, confirm that you want to enter the quiz as the student.
6. Let's go ahead and submit all of the saved responses by clicking on the **Go To Submit Quiz** button.
7. Click on the **Submit Quiz** button.
8. Finally, verify that you'd like to submit the quiz by clicking on the **Yes, submit quiz** button.

How it works...

By entering the quiz as a student, we're able to see everything that has been saved in the attempt so far. Although we are only interested in submitting the attempt for the student, impersonating a student can be useful for answering questions relating to the quiz as well.

See also

▶ The *Deleting a student's quiz attempt* and *Giving students extra time on assessments* recipes

Minimizing cheating by randomizing questions and options

Unfortunately, there's no surefire method of preventing cheating on exams, whether they're electronic or paper-based. As online instructors, however, we do have many ways to help minimize cheating in our classes. Some instructors rely on essay questions and performance-based assessment, while others require exams be completed in a proctored environment or use special software, such as the **Respondus LockDown Browser**, to create a more secure online testing environment. The Desire2Learn Learning Suite also offers some useful tools for combating cheating.

Getting ready

We'll be creating a random multiple-choice exam using existing questions from
the question library. If you don't have items in your library, go ahead and take a few minutes
to create some now. For detailed instructions on importing existing quiz questions into the
question library, check out the *Copying quiz questions to the question library* recipe
in this chapter.

How to do it...

In this recipe, we'll learn how to randomize both the questions and question options to
create more secure assessments. Combined with other tools and techniques, this can go
a long way to deter cheating.

1. Access your course and navigate to the **Quizzes** tool.

2. Let's start by making sure that our question options are randomized. Click on the
   link to access the question library.

3. Locate a multiple-choice question, activate the context menu, and click on the
   Edit option. Then, make sure the **Randomize options** checkbox is selected:

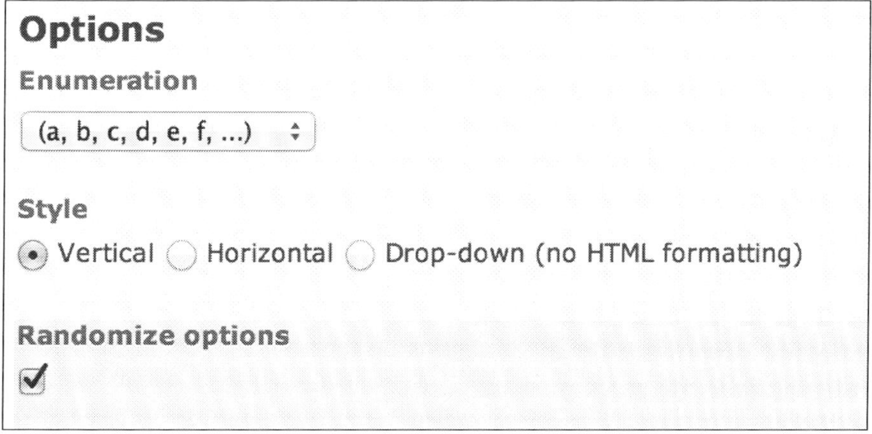

4. Click on **Save**. Repeat the same process for each multiple-choice question in
   the section.

5. Now that we have randomized the question options, let's create a quiz with random
   questions. Click on the **Done** button, then click on the **New Quiz** button.

6. Provide a name for the quiz in the **Properties** tab. Then, access the **Layout/
   Questions** tab.

7. Click on the **Add/Edit Question** button.

8. Click on the **New** button and choose **Random Section** option in the drop-down list.

9. Go ahead and provide a name for the section. Then, click on the **Save** button.

10. Access the section by clicking on its title in the list of quiz questions. Click on the **Import** button.

11. Identify the section of the library that contains the questions you want to import in the **Source Section** drop-down list.

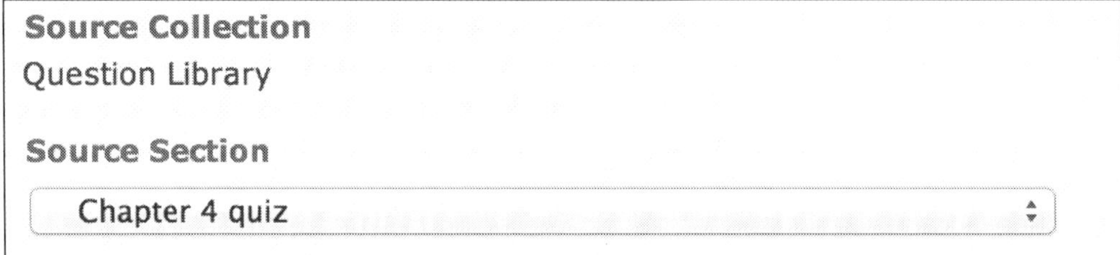

12. Select the checkbox next to each question you'd like to import, or select all the questions using the top-most checkbox.

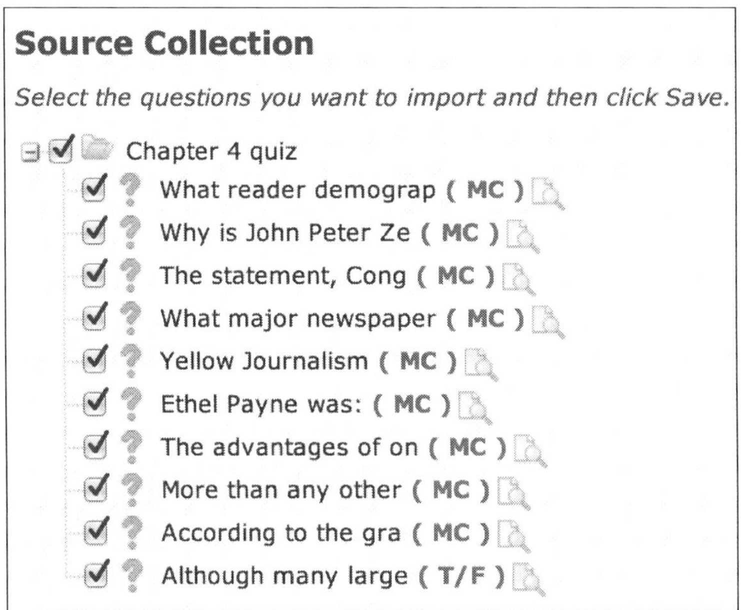

13. Click on the **Save** button.

14. At the top of the page, select the number of questions to display to each student and identify how many points each question will be worth.

[Import] [Save]

This is a random section. Select the number of questions to b

Questions per attempt: `10`

Points each: `1`

15. Click on **Save**.

How it works...

We began this recipe by verifying that all of the multiple-choice questions were set to display their options in a random order. This means that students taking the exam would not only receive their questions in a different order, but also the options within each question. If you choose this option, remember that you'll want to rewrite questions with options such as "all of the above" and "both a and b are correct."

After randomizing the question options, we created a new quiz and added a random section to it. The Learning Environment only allows you to randomize questions from the question library, so you have to either create questions in the question library or copy questions from the existing quizzes into it. In our example, we only created one random section, but you're able to add as many to an assessment as you like. You could, for example, create several random sections based on question difficulty. You could then pull in a specific number of questions from each section, which would guarantee that each student receives an equal number of easy and difficult questions.

See also

▶ The *Copying quiz questions to the question library* recipe

Correcting quiz questions

Quiz questions can be edited at any time by accessing either the **Add/Edit Questions** area or the question library (if you're using it). If a question exists in multiple locations within the same course, then you're given the option to update the question everywhere it appears. Altering questions in this manner, however, does not affect questions in on-going or completed quiz attempts. Once a student begins a quiz, their question versions are locked to the version that existed at the time they started the attempt.

Getting ready

In order to make this recipe easier to follow, we'll be using an example question shown in the following screenshot; feel free to modify the steps to work with your own questions:

When grading the question, it would appear as:

Who was the 16th President of the United States?

a) Sam Adams

b) George Washington

c) Abraham Lincoln

d) Bill Clinton

Notice that we have incorrectly identified the answer as **Sam Adams** even though the actual answer is **Abraham Lincoln**. In the following steps, we'll fix our mistake and make sure that students who already completed an attempt receive an appropriate credit for their work.

How to do it...

In this recipe, we will learn how to re-grade a question whose answer is incorrectly marked. We will give all students credit for the question answered correctly and also take away points from students who chose the incorrect (originally marked as correct) answer. You'll find this recipe useful for those (hopefully rare) times when you discover a problem with a question after students have already started taking an assessment.

1. Access your course and navigate to the **Quizzes** tool.

2. Locate the quiz that contains the incorrect question. Then, click on its title and access the **Layout/Questions** tab.

3. Click on the **Add/Edit Questions** button.

4. Choose the **Edit** option in the question's contextual menu.

5. Let's change the weight of **Sam Adams**, our incorrect answer, to 0. Then, change the weight for **Abraham Lincoln**, our correct answer, to 100.

6. Click on the **Save** button when finished. Click on the **Done** button on the **Edit Quiz** screen.

7. Activate the contextual menu next to the quiz name and choose the **Grade** option.

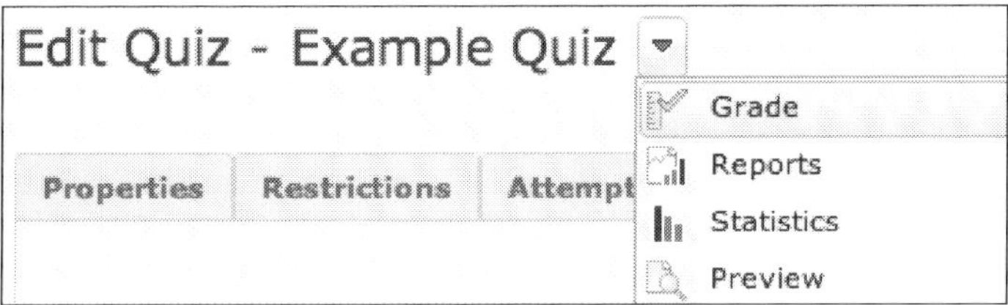

8. Navigate to the **Questions** tab and select the **Update All Attempts** option.

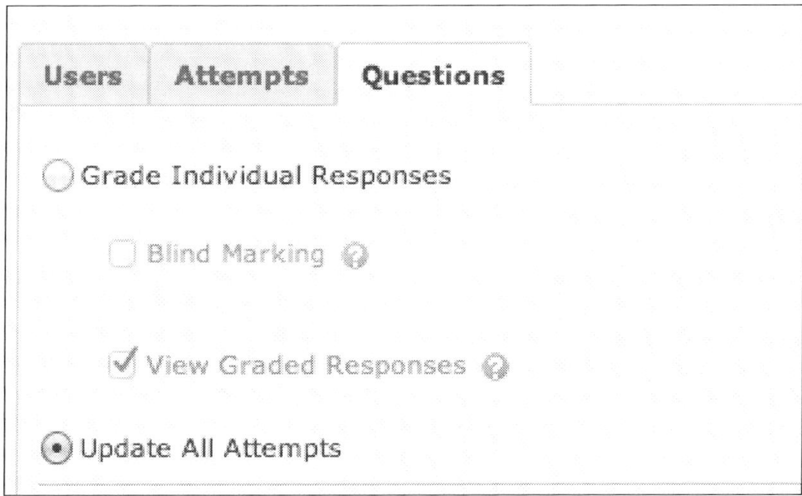

9. Click on the title of the question under the questions that are not in the quiz anymore.

10. Select the **Give to attempts with answer** option and choose **3** (the correct answer) from the drop-down list.

11. Enter the number of points the question is worth (let's say **1** point) in the text field:

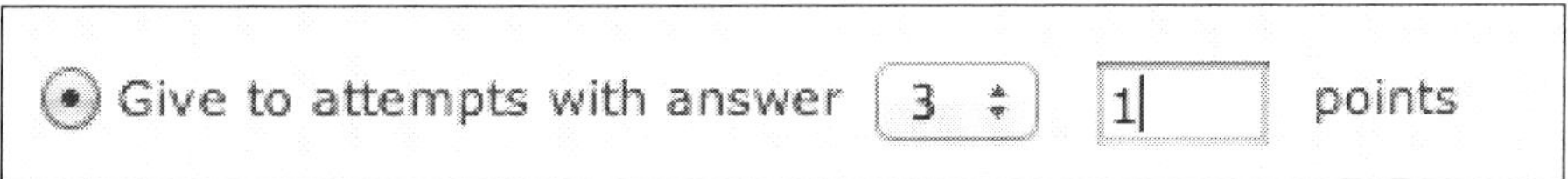

12. Click on the **Save** button.

13. Click on the **Yes** button in the dialog box that appears.

14. Select the **Give to students with answer** option again. This time, let's choose the first answer from the drop-down list and type 0 in the **points** text field.

15. Click on the **Save** button. When prompted, click on the **Yes** button.

How it works...

We began by accessing our quiz and fixing the question with the incorrect answer. By doing this, we ensured that future quiz attempts will present the correct version of the question. However, this doesn't do anything to fix the problem for students who have already started or completed an attempt. We need to access question details in order to make sure students receive proper credit for their answers.

In steps 8 to 13, we modified the old version of the question to give any student who chose the third option full credit for their response. At this point, we still have one small problem. Because of our original mistake when creating the question, anyone who incorrectly answered **Sam Adams** has also received full credit. We fixed this problem by giving everyone who chose the first answer 0 points in steps 14 to 15.

See also

▸ The *Deleting a student's quiz attempt* and *Submitting a quiz on behalf of a student* recipes

7

Collaboration and Participation

In this chapter, we will cover:

- Creating project/study groups
- Posting content for specific groups
- Creating a technical question forum
- Setting up a review session with Google Hangouts
- Facilitating collaborative note taking with Google Docs
- Monitoring specific discussion topics using notifications
- Monitoring participation
- Setting up Intelligent Agents
- Using the BCC field to keep the e-mail private

Introduction

Facilitating collaboration and monitoring participation in an online course can be difficult if you're more familiar working with students in a traditional, face-to-face environment. You can't, for example, scan the room for glazed-over eyes or see who's catching up on sleep during a lecture or activity. Building a sense of camaraderie between a group of students who may never hear or see each other may seem like an impossible task. Luckily, as educators in the Internet age, we have a variety of powerful collaboration tools at our disposal. In this chapter, we'll look at the ways in which you can use both Desire2Learn Learning Suite's built-in tools and some external services to facilitate teamwork and encourage participation in your online course.

We'll start off by using the Learning Suite's **Groups** tool to set up project/study groups, complete with members-only discussion forums and Dropbox folders. Then, we will use **Release Conditions** to post course content and even announcements to specific groups within the course. We'll also set up a special discussion forum where students can work together to answer each other's technical questions. While Desire2Learn Learning Suite's Groups and Discussion features are a great place to start, the other tools you would expect to see, such as text and video chat and collaborative document editing, are either missing entirely from the system or outdated when compared to similar Web 2.0 tools available on the Web.

Therefore, we will spend some time learning how to use tools, such as Google Docs and Google + to enhance collaboration in a Desire2Learn Learning Suite course. The concluding recipes present several different strategies for monitoring student participation—from creating notifications for discussion topics to setting up alerts using the Intelligent Agents tool.

Creating project/study groups

In this recipe, we will use Desire2Learn Learning Suite's Groups tool to create special work areas for a class project. Once the students are placed in groups, they can collaborate in team discussion forums, communicate with other team members using the e-mail tool, and submit team projects to a special Dropbox folder.

Getting ready

In order to complete this recipe, your role in the current course must have access to manage groups.

How to do it...

We will start by creating groups and configuring the system to randomly assign students to them. Then, we will take a look at how to set up group discussion areas and Dropbox folders. Finally, we'll make the Groups tool easily accessible by adding a link to the course's navbar.

1. Access your course and click on the **Edit Course** link.

2. Click on the **Groups** link under the **Learner Management** heading.

3. Click on the **New Category** link.

4. Provide a name for the **Group** category. I'm going to call mine `Group Projects`, but feel free to name yours to whatever you like.

5. Choose **Groups of #** in the **Enrollment Type** drop-down list. Then, limit the number of members in each group by typing a number in the **Number Of Users** field.

6. In the **Advanced Properties** section, check the **Auto-Enroll New Users** and **Randomize users in Groups** options.

7. Under the **Additional Options** header, check the boxes next to **Set Up Discussion Areas** and **Set Up Dropbox**. Then, click on the **Save** button. You may need to click on the **Expand the additional options** link in order to see these options.

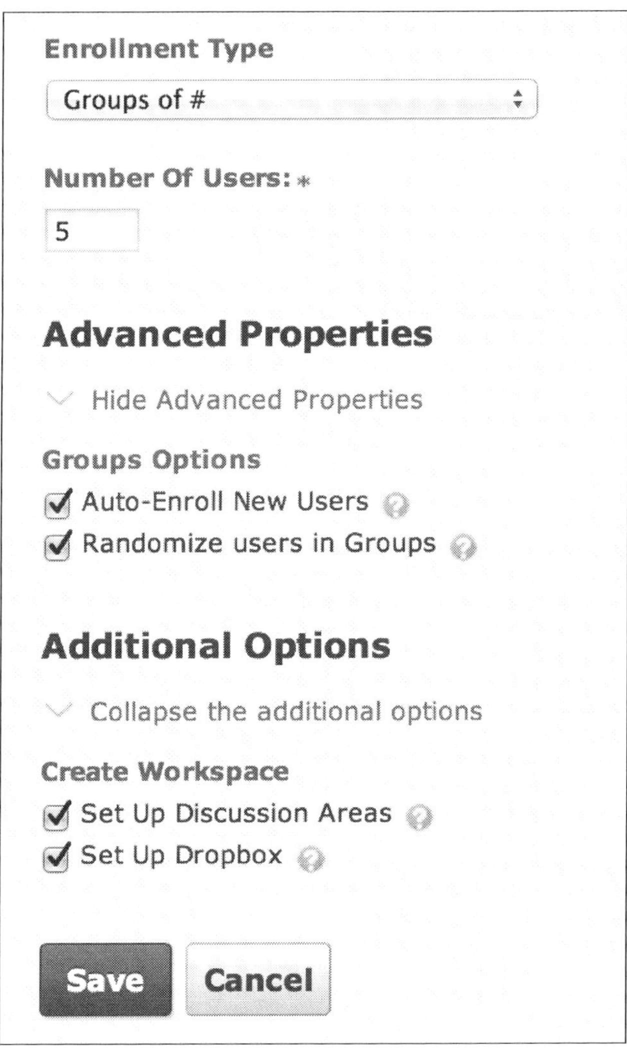

8. We're going to create a set of group-restricted topics. On the **Create Restricted Discussion Areas** screen, click on the **New Forum** link, provide a name for the forum in the pop-up window that appears, and click on the **Save** button:

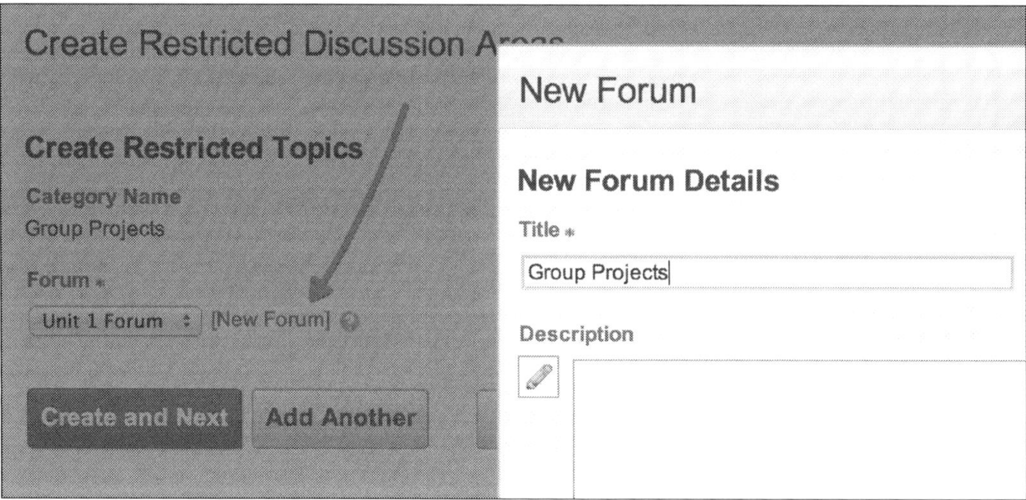

9. Click on the **Create and Next** button.

10. Now, we're going to create a group **Dropbox** folder. Provide a name for the folder in the text field. I am going to call mine **Group Projects**. If desired, associate the folder with an existing grade item or create a new one.

11. Click on the **Create** button. Then, click on the **Done** button.

How it works...

In the Desire2Learn Learning Environment, we use categories to organize our groups. Since we are creating a set of groups based on a class project, we called our category **Group Projects**. Although we're using the Groups tool for a large class project in this recipe, it also works well for small groups, such as peer review in writing classes.

Each group within the category is automatically assigned a generic name, such as `Group 1`, and `Group 2`. However, you can return to the Groups tool later on and provide a more descriptive name for each group if you'd like. We are only working with one category of groups at the moment, but you can create as many categories and groups for your course as you would like, and students can be enrolled on any number of class groups. That's a part of the great flexibility of the tool.

In this example, we chose to create groups of five students and have the system randomly assign each student to a group for us. We also selected the option to automatically add any new students to groups for us, which is especially useful if you're creating groups before the start of the semester. You probably noticed all of the other options for assigning students to groups. If you would prefer to manually select group members or allow students to join groups on their own, you can do so by selecting different options in the **Enrollment Type** drop-down list and under the **Advanced Properties** section.

There's more...

In step 7 of this recipe, we checked the options to automatically create an accompanying discussion topic and a Dropbox folder for each group. This is definitely a time saver when creating groups, but you may need to create additional forums and folders as the semester progresses. Rather than accessing the Groups tool, you can create these directly from the Discussion and Dropbox tools, although the process for each tool is slightly different.

Group discussion forums

In the following steps, we'll create a new discussion topic and limit its access to a specific group.

1. Start off by accessing the **Discussion** tool. Then, click on the **New** button and select the **Topic** option.

2. After providing a name, access the **Restrictions** tab and locate the **Group Restrictions** section. To restrict access to a group or multiple groups, check the box next to **Restrict this topic to the following groups** and click on the **Add Groups** button.

3. Select the groups you want to allow to access to the topic and click on the **Add** button.

4. Click on the **Save** button.

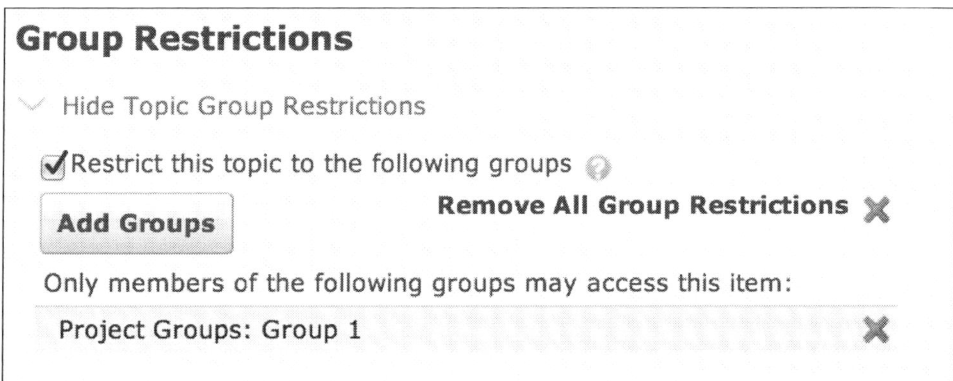

Group Dropbox folders

In order to create a group Dropbox folder, you'll need to choose the **Group submission** folder on the **Properties** tab. Once you create an individual submission folder, there's no way to make it a group submission folder.

1. Access the Dropbox tool, and click on the **New Folder** button.

2. Choose the **Group submission folder** option. Then, choose the group category from the drop-down list

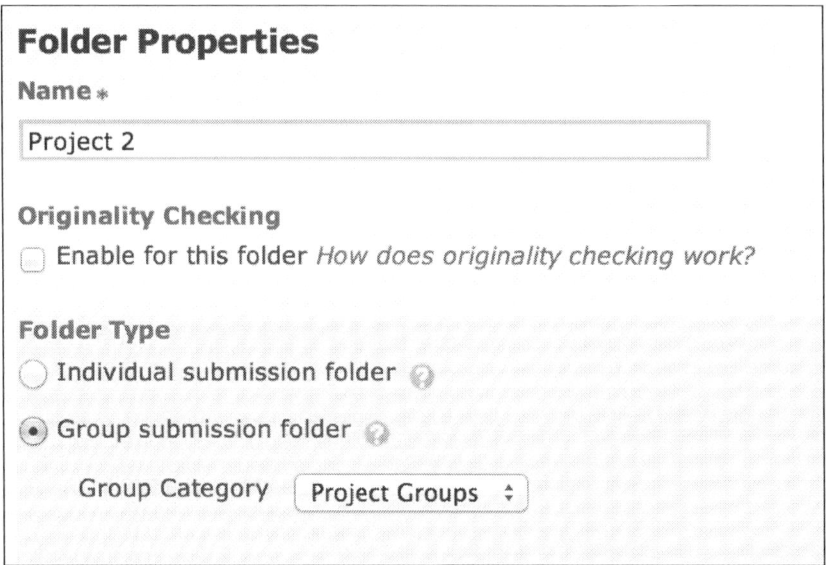

3. Click on **Save** button.

Group e-mail

Once you have created groups within a course, both instructors and students can use the filtering options in the Classlist tool to send email to all members of a group.

1. Access the **Classlist** tool and click on the **Email** button at the top of the page.

2. Choose **Groups** in the **View By** drop-down list.

3. Click on the **Apply** button.

4. Choose the group in the **Groups** drop-down list, and click on the **Apply** button again.

5. Click on the **Send Email** button at the bottom of the page, compose your message, and click on the **Send** button.

Adding a Groups link to the course navbar

By adding the Groups tool to the course navigation bar, you can give students a central location where they can e-mail other members of their group, collaborate in the group's discussion area, and submit their assignments to the Dropbox. If you're unsure about how to add a link to the course's navigation bar, please check out your school's support site or use the Learning Environment's built-in help system.

See also

> ▸ The *Posting content for specific groups* and *Monitoring specific discussion topics using notifications* recipes

Posting content for specific groups

In this recipe, we'll learn how to use Release Conditions to post announcements for specific groups within your course. We will also learn how you can combine multiple Release Conditions to make the tool even more powerful. While we will be focusing on the News tool in our example, many other tools in Desire2Learn's Learning Suite, such as Content and Quizzes, also use Release Conditions. You should be able to take what we cover in this recipe and apply it to any of these tools

Getting ready

We're going to be posting a news item that only a specific group of students will be able to see, so you'll need at least one category and group available in your course. Additionally, our news item will be a reminder that group evaluations need to be submitted to the Dropbox. If you don't already have a Dropbox folder created in your Desire2Learn Learning Suite course, go ahead and make one before following along with this recipe.

How to do it...

In the following steps, we will post a course news item reminding students to turn in their group projects. We will use release conditions to display the message to only those students who have not already submitted their work.

1. Access your course and navigate to the **News** tool.

2. Activate the context menu and choose the **New News Item** option.

3. Let's start by providing a headline in the text field. Then, type a message in the **Content** textbox that you only want to deliver to a certain group within the course.

4. Click on the **Create and Attach** button under the **Additional Release Conditions** heading.

5. In the **Condition Type** drop-down list, select **Group Enrollment**.

6. Choose one of your course groups from the Group drop-down list and click on the **Create** button.

7. Let's add another Release Condition by clicking on the **Create and Attach** button again.

8. This time, choose the **Submission to Dropbox** option in the **Condition Type** drop-down list.

9. Choose the correct assignment in the **Dropbox Folder** drop-down list. Click on the **Create** button.

10. Make sure the **All of the following conditions** option is selected in the drop-down list under the **Create and Attach** button.

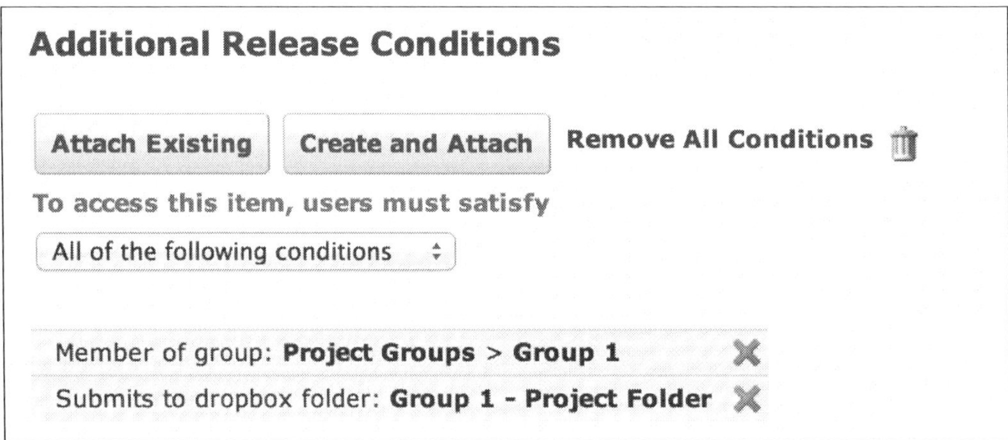

11. Click on the **Publish** button.

How it works...

We start off by creating a news item and making it visible to only a specific group. It's important to note that while we're working with the News tool in this example, you could use the same process for course content, quizzes, or any tool that supports release conditions. Since it doesn't make much sense to show the news item to students that have already submitted the assignment to the Dropbox, we added an additional release condition, eliminating anyone who has already turned in the assignment. Finally, we make sure that students would need to meet all of the release conditions before the news item could be shown.

You may be wondering why we didn't just look in the Dropbox tool and send an e-mail to anyone who hasn't submitted the assignment. While there's nothing wrong with that approach, we would need to revisit the Dropbox tool each time we wanted to send a reminder. With our approach, we set up the news item once and it remains visible to students until they submit their work.

See also

▶   The *Creating project/study groups* recipe

Creating a technical question forum

For inexperienced computer users, taking an online course can be quite intimidating. They may have difficulty completing general computer operations, or they may have questions about the Desire2Learn Learning Environment. In either case, you'd probably rather spend your days facilitating learning and building connections with students instead of replying to technical support e-mails. In this recipe, we will build a technical support forum to help answer some of these questions. Students will be able to post problems, provide answers, and even rate each other's responses. Although you're certainly welcome to visit the forum and submit your own comments, our goal is to create a tool where students will work with each other to solve basic technical problems.

Getting ready

In order to complete this recipe, your role in the current course must have permissions to create and modify discussion posts. In addition, the student role must be able to rate messages.

How to do it...

We're going to turn on the ability for students to rate responses while creating our technical help forum. By doing this, we will encourage students to vote for the best responses to common problems.

1. Access your course and navigate to the **Discussions** tool.

2. Click on the **New** button and choose the **Forum** option from the context menu.

3. Enter a title in the text field. Let's call our forum `Technical Questions`.

4. Go ahead and enter a short description in the **Description** text area.

5. Click on the **Save and Add Topic** button.

6. Now, let's add a topic to our newly created forum. I am going to call mine `Desire2Learn Questions`. Type a short description for the topic in the **Description** text area.

7. We are going to add one more topic to the forum before moving on. Click on **Save and New**.

8. Provide a title and description for this topic as well, just as we did in step 6. This time, let's call the topic `General Computer Questions`. Click on **Save** button.

9. Navigate back to the **Forums and Topics** list. Then, click on the **Settings** button in the upper-right corner of the main content area.

10. Under the **Org Unit Settings** header, make sure that the **Messages can be rated** option is selected:

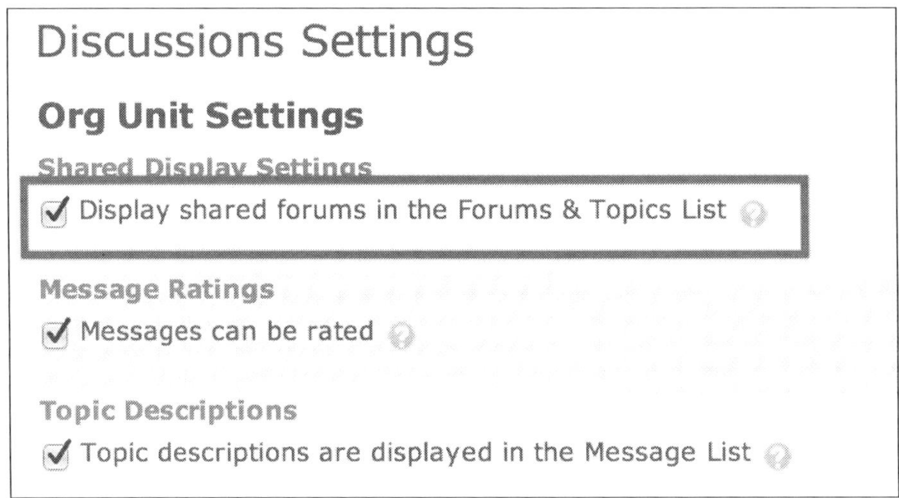

11. Click on the **Save** button.

How it works...

We begin this recipe by creating a forum to contain all of the technical support topics. Then, we add some discussion topics to help organize student questions. We create two initial topics; one for questions about the learning management system and another for general computer issues, but feel free to add as many topics as you'd like to the forum.

 Some institutions allow the student role to create discussion topics at the course level. If yours does, you may opt to let students create their own topics instead of setting up all the categories yourself.

After creating a forum and adding a few topics, make sure to visit the **Settings** area to verify that students in the course are able to rate messages. This will help determine which posts are helpful and which ones are not.

There's more...

Since we're allowing messages to be rated, we can use **Discussion Statistics** to identify which students are providing the most helpful replies. You can use this information to offer students extra credit or some other type of reward.

1. Start by navigating to the **Statistics** tab in the **Discussions** tool.

2. To view the statistics for each user, make sure that the **Users** tab is selected and click on the name of a student.

3. You can view their rating on each topic in the pop-up window that appears.

Forum/Topic Title	Total	Number of Messages				Average Rating ▾
		Authored	Read	Unapproved	Scored	
▣ Technical Questions	3	1	3	0	0	★★★★★
Desire2Learn Questions	3	1	3	0	0	★★★★★

See also

▶ The *Monitoring specific discussion topics using notifications* recipe

Setting up a review session with Google Hangouts

Google Hangout is a free, synchronous collaboration tool that you can use to host review sessions, meetings, and interviews for your online students. Once a Hangout is created, up to 10 participants can join the conversation, collaborate in documents, share their computer screens, and much more. Additionally, you can stream the Hangout to an associated YouTube channel, so that an unlimited number of participants can watch. You can even record the Hangout, so that individuals who are unable to attend the live session can view an archive at a later date.

Google Hangout offers some other advantages over similar tools such as Skype. For one, there's no application to install and maintain. After activating a **browser plugin**, you're ready to host or attend a session. Hangouts, as their name implies, are more informal than Web conferences or Skype calls. Hangout sessions are more like rooms than conferences or calls; once you create a Hangout, folks are free to come and go as they please.

Getting ready

You are going to need a Google account in order to complete this recipe. Additionally, you'll want to verify your YouTube account to enable longer recording sessions. Head over to `http://accounts.google.com` and create an account, if you don't already have one. Since we will be web conferencing, you will need a web camera and a microphone as well.

Please check with your institution's policies on using external services, such as Google Hangouts, before completing this recipe. Some schools choose to limit the access to third-party services. Additionally, your school may have preferred vendors for web conferencing and online collaboration, including solutions available from Desire2Learn.

How to do it...

In this recipe, we will use Google Hangouts to host a review session for an upcoming exam. We will also stream the session to our YouTube channel, embed it in a Desire2Learn Learning Suite course, and create an archive of everything for later viewing.

1. Open your web browser and navigate to `https://plus.google.com`.

2. Click on the **Sign in** link, then provide your username and password and click on the **Sign in** button.

3. If you haven't used Google+ before, you'll be prompted to add some people you know to your circles. We can skip that for now by clicking on the **Continue** button until you arrive at the Google+ **Home** screen.

4. Click on the **Hangouts** button in the left column of the page.

5. Click on the **Start Hangout** button at the top of the page.

6. Click on the **X in the Your Circles** tag, and provide a name for the hangout.

7. Then, select the **Enable Hangouts on Air** checkbox. If prompted to accept the terms and conditions, go ahead and do so:

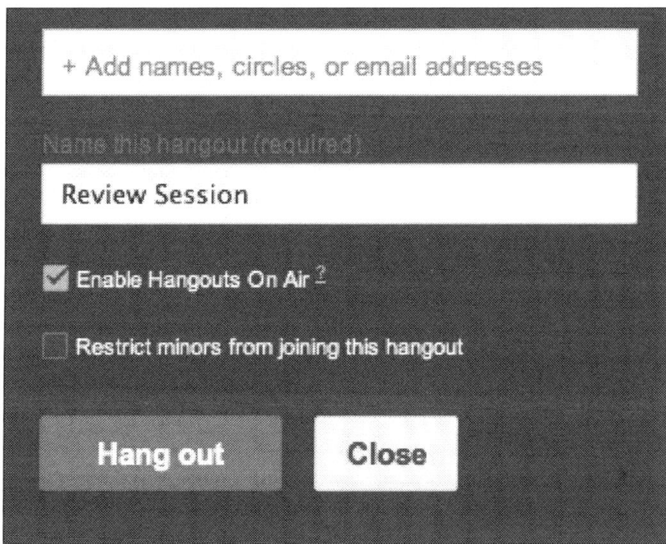

8. Click on the **Hang out** button.

9. Click on the **Embed** link at the top of the page. Then, copy the URL to your clipboard and open a new tab in your browser:

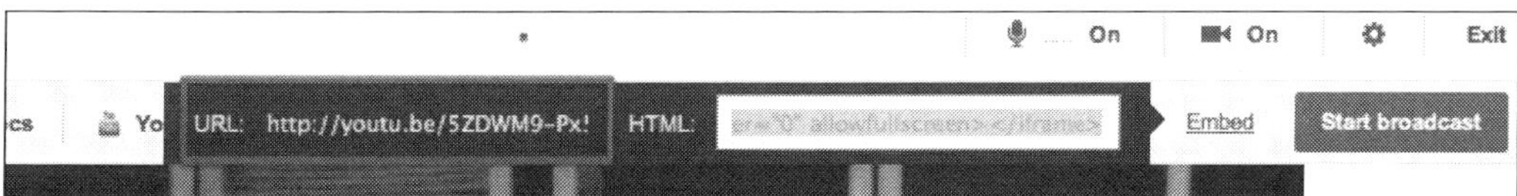

10. In you new tab, access the **News** section for one of your online courses.

11. Activate the context menu at the top of the **News** widget, and choose the **New News Item** option. Provide a headline for the Hangout and click on the **Insert Stuff** button in the toolbar.

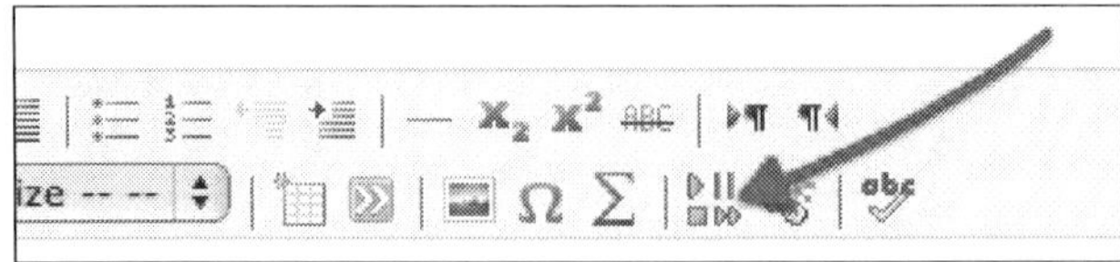

12. Choose the **Insert Link** option in the left column, and paste the URL we copied earlier into the text field in the right side of the page:

13. Click on the **Next** button. Then, click on the **Insert** button.

14. Click on the **Publish** button to create your news item.

15. In your web browser, access your previous tab to return to your Hangout session. Then click on the **Start broadcast** button. Once the next page loads, your session is live.

16. When the session starts, you will be sharing a video stream from your webcam with any other participants. You can use the other options to collaborate on documents, watch YouTube videos, and more

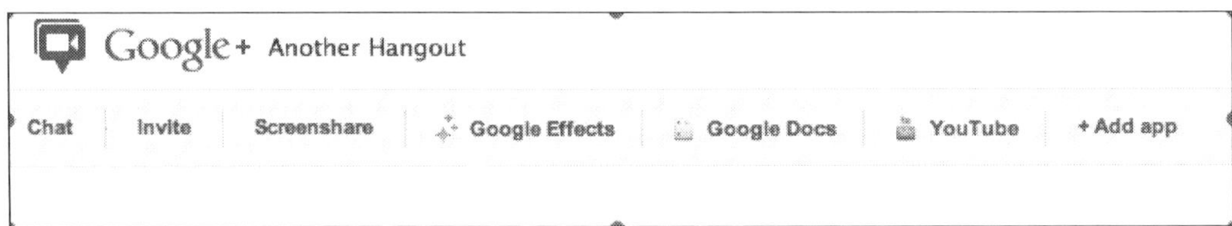

17. Click on the **Exit** link to leave the session when you're finished.

How it works...

Google + uses the concept of **circles** to help you organize your contacts into groups. A contact can be placed in any number of circles, and when you share content or create hangouts, you choose which circles have access to it. If your students use Google +, you may want to create a circle for each of your classes to enable easy sharing with those individuals.

Once you are logged in to Google+, you can create new Hangout sessions by clicking on the **Hangout** button. By default, sessions are shared with individuals in all of your circles. You can change that by deleting the **Your Circles** option and manually adding the names or circles to which you want to give access.

By selecting the **Enable Hangouts On Air** checkbox, your session will be both recorded and streamed live to your YouTube channel. Hangouts On Air also gives us the option to embed the live stream on a website. In our case, that's our Desire2Learn Learning Suite course homepage. Once the session is created, we should copy the URL for the live stream and add it to our course using the **Insert Stuff** button. Anyone viewing the page during the Hangout will see the video live, while anyone visiting afterwards will be shown an archived version saved on your YouTube channel.

Understanding the privacy and safety issues on any social network is extremely important. In addition to following your school's official policy for using external services, such as Google + and YouTube, be sure to take a look at the terms of service before using them in your course. I also recommend visiting the Google + Safety center, `http://www.google.com/intl/en/+/safety/`, for useful tips for educators.

See also

> ▸ The *Facilitating collaborative note taking with Google Docs* recipe

Facilitating collaborative note taking with Google Docs

Google Docs is a suite of free, online tools for creating and sharing documents, spreadsheets, presentations, and more. Since the tool is web-based, any document created in or uploaded to the service is accessible from any web-enabled computer or mobile device. This means that neither you nor your students need to install expensive programs in order to be able to view or edit the documents. By default, documents created using the service are visible only to the author; however, items can be easily shared with individual contacts or even made publically available on the Internet.

Getting ready

You will need a Google account in order to create Google Documents. If you don't already have an account, head over to `http://accounts.google.com` to create one before beginning this recipe. As always, check your school's official policies regarding the use of external services such as Google Docs.

How to do it...

In this recipe, we'll create a collaborative work area where students in our course can work together to create class notes. We'll then link to the document from within the Content tool of our Desire2Learn Learning Suite course, so that the documents can be easily accessed at any time.

1. Let's start by opening a web browser and navigating to `http://docs.google.com`.

2. Click on the **Sign in** button, then provide the login credentials for your Google account, and click on the **Sign in** button.

3. Click on the **Create** button and choose the **Folder** option. When prompted, provide a name for the folder (`Class Notes`) and click on **Create**.

4. Now that we have a folder, let's add a new document to it by clicking on the **Create** button again and choosing the **Document** option this time.

5. Rename the document by clicking on the **Untitled document** text in the upper-left corner of the screen. Provide a new name for the document in the text field and click on the **OK** button. I'm calling mine `Class Notes - Unit 1`, but feel free to name yours whatever you'd like.

6. At the moment, no one else is able to access the document. Let's change that by clicking on the **Share** button in the upper-right corner of the screen.

7. Click on the **Change** link under the **Who has access** heading.

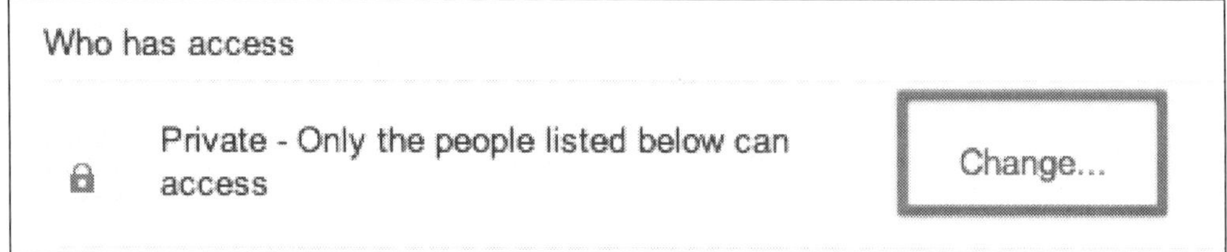

8. Under **Visibility options**, select **Anyone with the link**. Then, choose the **Can edit** option in the **Access** drop-down list

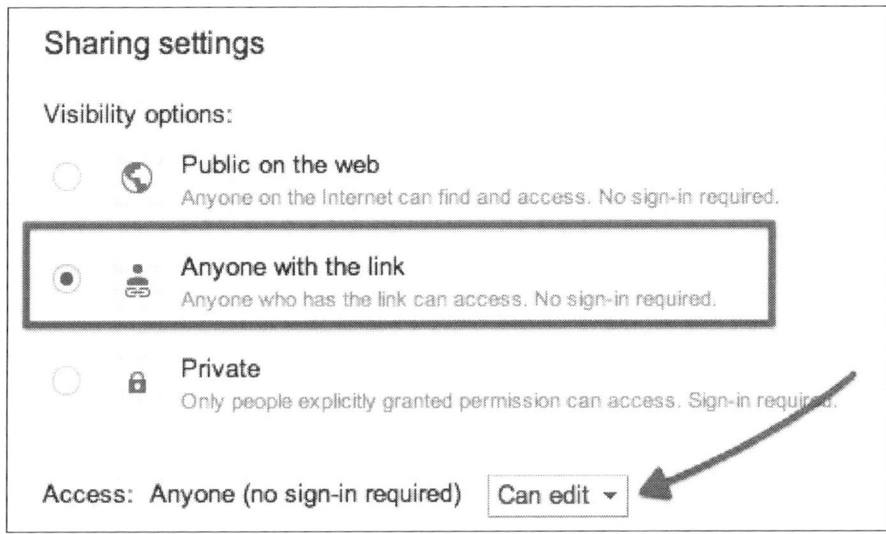

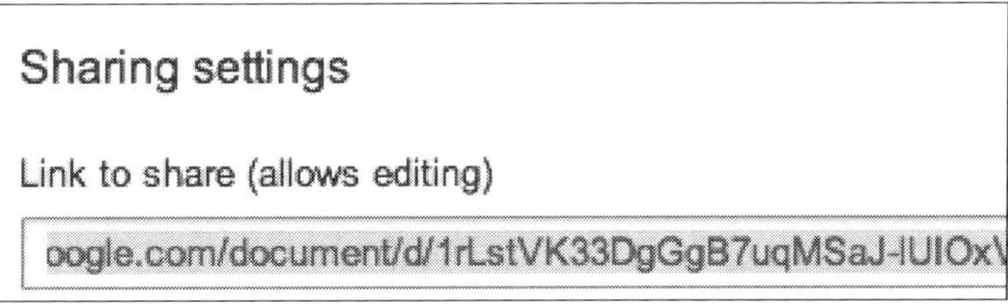

9. Click on the **Save** button. Copy the document's URL from the link to share the text field at the top of the page. Then, click on the **Done** button.

10. Go ahead and open a new tab in your browser and access the homepage for your Desire2Learn Learning Suite course.

11. Navigate to the **Content** area, and click on the **Add Content** button. Select the **New Module** option.

12. Let's call our new module `Course Notes`. Go ahead and type the title in the text field and click on the **Save** button.

13. Now, let's create a link to the Google Document by activating the context menu to the right of our new module and clicking on the **New Quicklink** option.

14. Choose **Course Notes** in the **Parent Module** drop-down menu. Type `Class Notes - Unit 1` for the title.

15. Paste the link to the Google Document in the URL text field and check the option to preview/view the content topic in a new window or tab.

16. Click on **Save**.

How it works...

We begin by accessing Google Docs, creating a new folder, and adding our first document to the folder. Although we chose to create all of our materials within the system, you can also upload the existing Microsoft Office documents if you prefer—just click on the **Upload** icon next to the **Create** button to select the file you'd like to upload.

Once you create and rename our document, visit the **Share** settings in order to make the document available (and editable) to anyone with a link. With this option, the document won't be indexed by search engines, but anyone with the link would be able to modify its contents. If you'd rather limit the access to just the students in your course, you do have the option of providing a list of e-mail addresses at the bottom of the **Share Settings** screen. However, this would require students to log in to Google Docs in order to access the documents, so I have chosen not to go down that route in our example. After modifying the sharing options for the document, we copied and pasted its URL into a new topic in our Desire2Learn Learning Suite course.

See also

- The *Using Google Docs to allow multiple download formats* recipe in *Chapter 3, Getting Materials into Your Course*

Monitoring specific discussion topics using notifications

Desire2Learn Learning Suite's **notification** feature allows students to sign up to receive alerts for important activities within your course. They can, for example, get e-mail or **text message (SMS)** alerts when new items are posted or before important assignments are due.

Getting ready

In order to complete this recipe, your role within the course needs to have permissions to receive notifications.

How to do it...

In this recipe, we'll set up notifications to help us keep a track of the important discussion forums and topics. By providing an e-mail address in **notification preferences** and subscribing to a **discussion** thread, we will instantly receive an e-mail any time a student posts or replies to a message. While you probably don't want to subscribe to all topics in your forum, keeping a track of important topics can be helpful at times.

1. Let's start by setting up notifications for your account. In your Web browser, log in to the system, activate your personal menu in the minibar. and click on the **Notifications** link.

2. Click on the **Enable email notifications** link. For now, let's choose the option to receive notifications at the system specified e-mail address. Click on the **Save** button when finished.

3. Since we are only interested in receiving alerts for discussion topics at this time, make sure the **Email** option for **Discussions** is checked. Click on the **Save** button at the bottom of the screen.

4. Now that we've turned on notifications, let's subscribe to some discussion topics. Access one of your courses and navigate to the **Discussions** tool.

5. Locate a topic for which you'd like to receive notifications of new the postings. Click on the star icon to the left of the thread to subscribe to it.

6. In the **Notification Frequency** drop-down list, choose the **Send me an instant notification** option. Then, click on the **Subscribe** button.

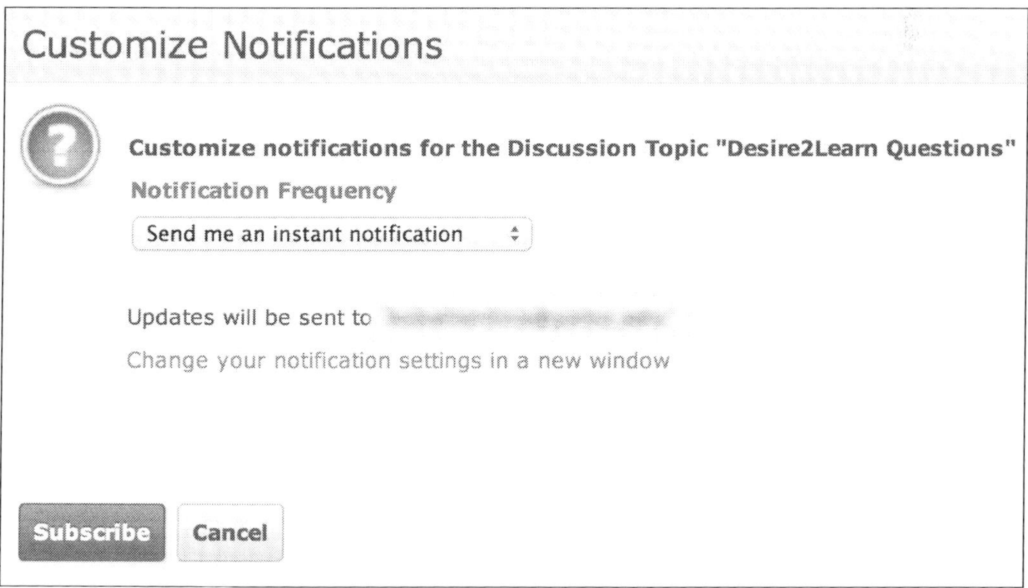

7. To view and manage all of your subscriptions, click on the **Subscriptions** tab in the **Discussions** tool. You can unsubscribe by clicking on the **Unsubscribe** link or by switching between the instant and summary notification options in the **Notification Frequency** area:

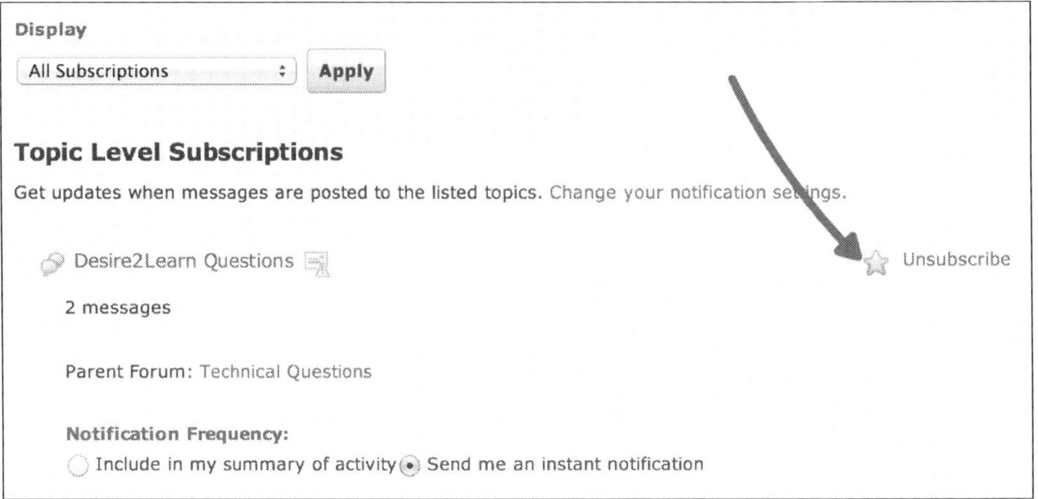

How it works...

We begin by setting up our Notification preferences. In this recipe, we chose the option to receive notifications to the system-specified e-mail address, although you're welcome to provide an external e-mail address if you prefer instant notifications be sent to a personal account. You may have also noticed the option to configure your mobile phone to receive alerts. At this time, alerts for the Discussions tool can only by sent via e-mails, so we didn't bother setting that up right now.

Once you enable notifications for your account, visit the **Discussions** tool to subscribe to a topic. Clicking the star icon to the left of a topic title toggles a subscription on and off; you can subscribe to a topic by clicking on an empty star icon or unsubscribe by clicking on the icon again at a later date. The **Subscriptions** tab in the **Discussion Areas** widget gives a summary of all current subscriptions along with the option to adjust the notification frequency or drop a subscription.

See also

▶ The *Monitoring participation* recipe

Monitoring participation

The Learning Environment's **View Progress** tool, available from the Classlist course, is a great way to monitor student activity in a course. You can find out when students access the system, track which items they visit in the Content and Discussions tools, and so on.

How to do it...

In this recipe, we'll use the Learning Environment's **Track User Progress** function to monitor student participation in several key areas of our online course. We will view the system login history to make sure which students were accessing the system. Then, we'll view the content statistics to determine the amount of time a selected student has spent viewing the items within the Content tool. Finally, we'll use Track User Progress to view a student's participation in the course's Discussions tool.

1. Access the **Classlist** tool in one of your courses.

2. Locate a student whose participation you'd like to assess. Activate the context menu for the student and choose the **View progress** option:

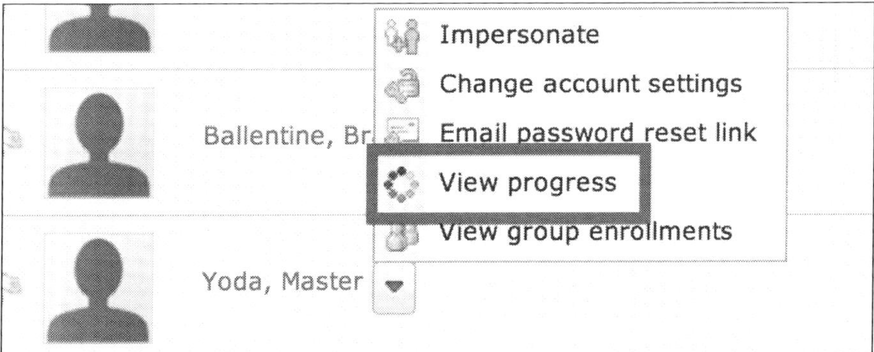

3. Let's start by viewing the student's system login history. In the **Progress Selection** section, click on the **Change** button. Choose **System Login History** in the **Tool** drop-down list and click on the **Apply** button:

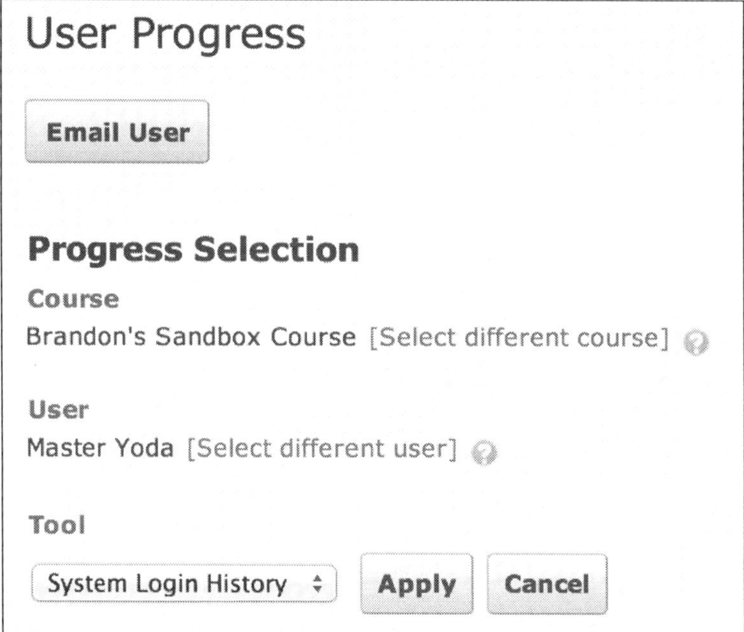

4. Under the **Login Summary** heading, you'll now see the last date when the student accessed your course along with some system-wide login information.

5. Let's see how much time our student spends in the content section of the course. Go ahead and click on the **Change** button again, this time selecting the **Course Content** option in the drop-down list.

6. Don't forget to Click on the **Apply** button after making your selection.

7. The **Content Summary** section gives us a quick look at how much time our student has spent viewing the course materials. You can determine the amount of time this student has spent viewing content and compare that with the class average by viewing the statistics in the **Content Details** section.

8. Let's see how active our student has been in the **Discussion** tool. Go ahead and click on the **Change** button one more time. Choose the **Discussions** option in the drop-down list and click on the **Apply** button.

9. We can view the number of topics the student has contributed to the discussion forum along with the number of posts he or she has read in the **Discussions Summary** section. For more detailed information, take a look at the **Discussions Details** section.

How it works...

You access the Track User Progress tool by clicking on the icon on the course's class list. From there, you can view the information on a variety of different tools by selecting the options in the **Progress Selection** drop-down list and clicking on the **Apply** button. It's important to note that the login history, with the exception of **Last Course Access**, refers to the system login and not access to the current course offering. To view the progress for other students, you can either return to the Classlist or click on the **Select different user** link and search for another student in the course.

See also

> ▸ The *Monitoring specific discussion topics using notifications* recipe

Setting up Intelligent Agents

Intelligent Agents is an extremely flexible tool used to monitor a Desire2Learn Learning Suite course for a designated criteria. As an instructor, you define which activities you would like to track; login history, scores on assessments, and so on. When students meet the defined criteria, the system automatically sends an e-mail. Because of its flexibility, you can use the tool to both recognize student activity and warn of potential problems.

Getting ready

In order to complete this recipe, your role in the current course needs to have access to the Intelligent Agents tool.

How to do it...

In this tutorial, we'll use the Intelligent Agents tool to warn students when they have not visited the course in a week. We'll also send the message to ourselves, so that we can attempt to follow-up with students before they fall too far behind in the course.

1. Access the **Edit Course** tool in your course.

2. Click on the **Intelligent Agents** link under the **Communication** heading.

3. Click on the **New** button at the top of the page to create a new Intelligent Agent.

4. We need to provide a name for our agent in the **Agent Name** field. Let's call ours `No login - 7 days`.

5. Go ahead and select the **Agent is enabled** option to activate our agent.

6. Check the **Take action when the following course activity criteria are satisfied** option under the **Course Activity** heading.

7. Select the top radio button. Then, type a 7 in the text field for that option.

Course Activity

Take action when the following course activity criteria are satisfied

Course Activity

- User has not accessed course for at least 7 day(s)
- User has accessed course during the past day(s)

8. In the **Agent Action** section, select **Take action every time the agent is evaluated and the agent's criteria are satisfied for a user** option.

9. Now let's set a schedule for our agent. Check the **Use Schedule** option, and then click on the **Update Schedule** button.

10. Since we want to send weekly reminders, change the **Repeats** drop-down list to **Weekly**, set the action to repeat every one week, and select the **Monday** option

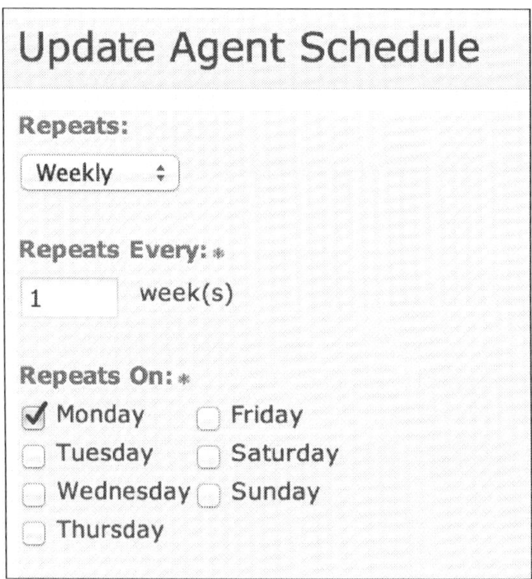

11. Go ahead and set the start and end dates for the agent in the **Schedule Dates** section. Make sure that the end date is set to no later than the last day of the semester. Then, click on the **Update** button.

12. Let's send a reminder to both ourselves as well as the student who hasn't accessed the course. Go ahead and enter your e-mail address in the **Cc:** field. Type `{InitiatingUser}` in the **To:** field.

13. In the **Email Subject** text field, type `Class participation - {OrgUnitName}`.

14. In the **Message** text area, type: `Hi {InitiatingUserFirstName}, Your have received this message because you have not accessed {OrgUnitName} in at least 7 days. Click here to access the course - {LoginPath}.`

15. Click on the **Save** button.

How it works...

We start this recipe by creating a new Intelligent Agent and making it active. Since we're interested in identifying students who may be in danger of falling behind, make sure to check the option when students fail to access the course for a period of seven days.

In the **Action Repetition** section, choose the option to perform the action each time a student fails to access the course within a seven-day period. Make sure to also specify that the agent should be evaluated weekly. This way, you don't need to remember to access the Intelligent Agent tool each week and manually trigger the agent. It's also a good idea to schedule an end date for the agent that falls on or before the end of the semester; otherwise, you'll continue receiving e-mails after students lose access to the course at the end of the semester.

You can use special system variables, called **replace strings**, to send customized messages to each student. The `{InitiatingUser}` string in the **To:** field is replaced with the e-mail address for each student who meets the agent's criteria. The `{InitiatingUserFirstName}` and `{OrgUnitName}` strings are replaced with the student's first name and name of the course, respectively. Feel free to click on the **What special e-mail addresses can I use?** and **What replace strings can I use in the subject and message?** links to view all available replace strings. When composing your message, you can use the **Insert Replace String** button to easily add replace strings to your e-mail:

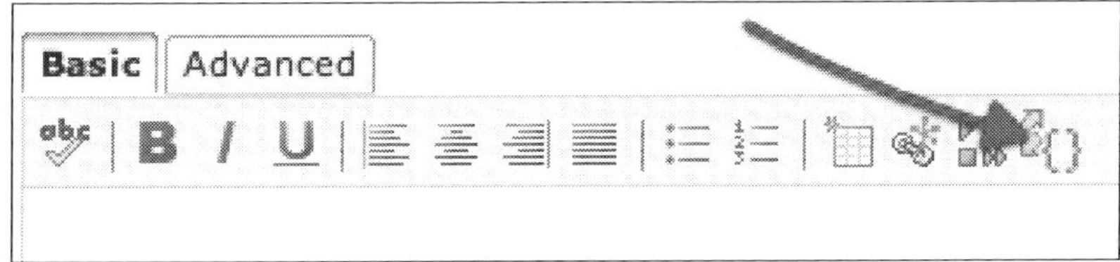

See also

> ▶ The *Posting content for specific groups, Monitoring specific discussion topics using notifications*, and *Monitoring participation* recipes

> ▶ The *Using system variables to create customized content* recipe in *Chapter 2, Personalizing your course*

Using the BCC field to keep the e-mail private

The **Email Selected Users** functionality in the Classlist tool makes it easy to send messages to multiple recipients within a Desire2Learn Learning Suite course. While this is a great way of sending general announcements, such as schedule changes and upcoming assignment due dates, you'll want to be careful not to violate your students' privacy when sending other types of messages. For example, you wouldn't want to reach out to several students who performed poorly on a particular assessment by adding multiple names to the **To:** field, because each recipient of the message would be able to view the addresses of every other recipient. In situations such as this, you would be better off adding addresses to the **Bcc:** field in order to help keep the e-mail private.

Getting ready

This recipe assumes that your organization is using D2L's internal e-mail system and has configured selected addresses to be added to the **To:** field.

How to do it...

In this brief recipe, we'll learn how to help keep the e-mail private by using the **Bcc:** field.

1. Access your D2L course and navigate to the **Classlist** tool.

2. Check the boxes next to the name of each student that you'd like to send e-mails to.

3. Click on the **Email selected users in a new window** button at the top of the list of names

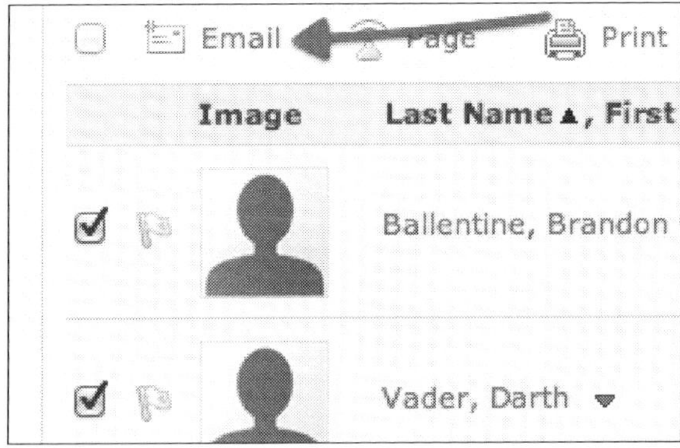

4. Copy the addresses from the **To:** field and paste them in the **Bcc:** field. Then, type your own name in the **To:** field.

5. Provide a subject for your message in the **Subject** text field and compose your message in the HTML editor.

6. Click on the **Send** button when done.

How it works...

Begin by selecting the checkboxes next to the names of each student we want to receive our message. After clicking the **Email** icon, copy all of the e-mail addresses from the **To:** field and paste them in the **Bcc:**, or blind carbon copy, field. Unlike the **To:** or **Cc:** (carbon copy) options, blind carbon copy indicates that individual recipients are unable to see the names of all other recipients of the message.

It's important to note that your school's Desire2Learn administrator may have already changed the default functionality of the tool to automatically add addresses to the **Bcc:** field. If this is the case, then you don't need to worry about the steps described in this recipe; all the work has already been done for you.

8

Working with the Grades Tool

In this chapter, we will cover the following recipes:

- Dropping the lowest item in a grade book category
- Displaying an on-going total or mid-term report
- Hiding grade items from students
- Setting up your grades view to minimize scrolling
- Creating a new letter grade scheme
- Calculating and releasing final grades
- Previewing grades from a student's perspective
- Viewing grades for students who have withdrawn from a course
- Exporting a backup copy of your grades

Introduction

By utilizing the **Grades** tool in your online courses, you give students the benefit of 24/7 access to their scores on assignments and assessments. In addition, the Grades tool alleviates many of the common frustrations that you're likely to experience in creating and maintaining a traditional paper-based grade book. While there's a little doubt the Grades tool can be a useful addition to any course, it's also one of the most difficult tools to manage.

This chapter includes recipes that will help you become more productive with the Grades tool. We start with some time-saving tips for dropping the lowest score within a gradebook category, displaying a running total of points earned in the course, and hiding pop quizzes from the student view. We then discuss how to modify your display settings to minimize scrolling and look at how you can create and assign custom grade schemes. We wrap up the chapter by learning how to calculate and display final grades to the students as well as how you can export an archive of your students' scores at the end of the semester.

Dropping the lowest item in a gradebook category

In this recipe, we'll learn how to drop the lowest grade(s) from a given category in your gradebook. You can use this technique to drop a student's lowest quiz or homework score or allow students to pick assignments from several available options – completing 5 or 10 available assignments, for example. While you can achieve the same result using a formula in an electronic spreadsheet or performing calculations manually in a paper-based gradebook, using categories in the Learning Environment's Grades tool greatly simplifies the process. Best of all, the tool automatically updates the dropped items as more grades are entered!

Getting ready

In order to complete this recipe, you're going to need to have access to the Grades tool in a Desire2Learn Learning Suite course. We'll be using a points-based grade system in the following example, but you're welcome to adjust the steps for a weighted grade system; the steps are very similar.

How to do it...

In the following steps, we will create a new gradebook category and configure the system to automatically drop each student's lowest attempt.

1. Access your D2L course and navigate to the **Grades** tool.

2. Navigate to the **Manage Grades** area. Then, click on the **New** button and choose the **Category** option.

3. Let's name our new category by typing `Quizzes` in the **Name** field.

4. Make sure that the **Distribute points across all items** option is checked.

5. If necessary, change the number of points per item to match your course syllabus. In this example, I want each quiz to be worth 100 points, so I have changed the default `10` points to `100`.

6. Since we're dropping the lowest quiz score for each student, type a `1` in the text field next to the **Number of lowest non-bonus items to drop for each user** option.

Distribution: ☑ Distribute points across all items ⊚

100	Points per item ⊚
0	Number of highest non-bonus items to drop for each user ⊚
1	Number of lowest non-bonus items to drop for each user ⊚

7. Click on the **Save** button.

How it works...

In addition to helping keep your grade book organized, you can use categories to automatically drop a specific number of the lowest or highest scores within a certain group of assignments. In order to make use of this feature, all items in the category need to be worth the same number of points or need to be weighted equally, depending on whether you are using a points-based grade book or a weighted one.

After distributing points evenly, we entered the number of items to drop from the category. In our example, we chose to drop only the lowest item in the category, but you can be more creative in your own class. For example, you could allow students to choose to complete five of a possible ten assignments. All you'd need to do is assign all the ten items to the category and make sure to drop the lowest five items.

Once you set up the category, your work is done. The Grades tool will automatically drop the lowest items for you. Dropped grades are marked with an exclamation mark in your grade book:

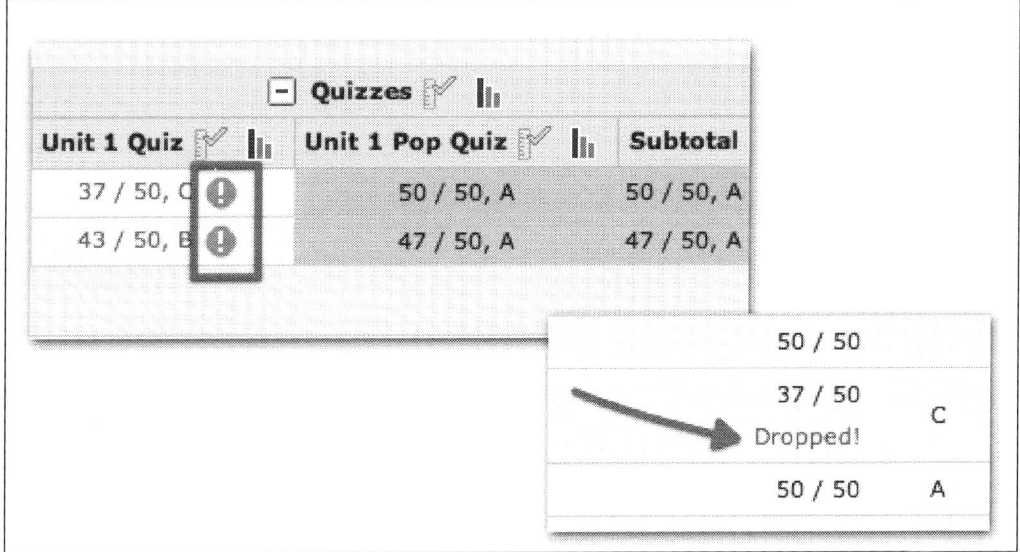

▶ The *Previewing grades from a student's perspective* recipe

Displaying an on-going total or mid-term report

Although students can view their performance on individual grade items, determining their current status in the course often requires a little math. In this recipe, we'll make life easier for our students by creating a special item in the grade book that displays the points earned so far as well as the total available points. This item will give students an easy way to find out how they're doing in the course at any given time in the semester.

Getting ready

The **Calculated** grade item type is based on points, so it will be most useful if your course utilizes a points-based grade system. You're welcome to follow along even if you use a weighted grade book or one based on a custom formula; just be aware that the number displayed may differ dramatically from a student's actual grade for the course.

How to do it...

In this recipe, we'll create a new calculated grade item that displays the total number of points earned for each student in the course.

1. Access your course and navigate to the **Grades** tool.

2. Click on to the **Manage Grades** link. Next, click on the **New** button and select the **Item** option from the drop-down list.

3. Choose the **Calculated** option in the list of available grade item types.

4. Since we're showing students the total number of accumulated points at any given time in the semester, let's type `Total Points Earned` in the **Name** text field.

5. In the **Grade Item to Include** section, select the checkbox next to each item that needs to be included in the calculation. Make sure to uncheck any assignment that you have not yet graded.

6. Click on the **Save** button.

How it works...

Displaying an on-going total is as simple as adding a new Calculated grade item to the course. In step 5, we checked the boxes next to each item to include in the initial calculation. Make sure to select the checkboxes next to each grade item that you've graded so far.

There's more...

In order to keep the running total up to date, you will need to revisit the **Manage Grades** area and add new items to the calculation as you enter grades for new assignments.

1. From the **Grades** tool, navigate to **Manage Grades** and click on the name of the calculated grade item.

2. Select the checkbox next to the new grade item(s) to include in the **Total Points Earned** calculation.

3. Click on the **Save** button.

See also

▶ The *Calculating and releasing final grades* and *Previewing grades from a student's perspective* recipes

Hiding grade items from students

The ability for students to log in and view their grades at any time is one of the greatest features of the Grades tool. While easy, 24-hour access to the tool helps the students keep up with their performance and frees the instructors from answering many grade-related queries. It also makes keeping a pop quiz as a secret a little difficult, especially if you create all your grade items at the beginning of the semester.

Getting ready

In order to complete this recipe, your role in the current course will need to have permissions to create and edit grade items.

How to do it...

In the following steps, we'll learn how to modify a grade item's restrictions to hide it from the student view.

1. Access your D2L course and navigate to the **Grades** tool.

2. Click on the **Manage Grades** link.

3. Let's create a new pop quiz grade item. Start by clicking on the **New** button at the top of the page. Then, choose the **Item** option from the drop-down list.

4. Click on the **Numeric** link.

5. Type a name for the pop quiz in the **Name** text field. If necessary, go ahead and choose a category and then adjust the maximum points for the grade item.

6. Access the **Restrictions** tab. Then, select the **Grade item is visible for a specific date range** radio button.

7. Select the **Has Start Date** checkbox and choose a start date after the pop quiz:

8. Make sure the **Has End Date** and **Display in Calendar** options remain unchecked.

9. Click on the **Save** button.

How it works...

After you create a new grade item, visit the **Restrictions** tab and modify the item's visibility to hide it from your students. You can determine when the item should appear for the students in the student grade book by selecting the **Grade item is visible for a specific date range** option and providing a start date. In this recipe, we chose not to enter an end date, since we want the item to remain visible from the start date through the end of the semester.

You may be wondering why we didn't simply select **Hide this grade item**. If we had selected that option, we would need to revisit the grade item in the future to make it visible to the students. Although you're welcome to do that, it's preferable to set up everything when creating the item.

See also

▶ The *Previewing grades from a student's perspective* recipe

Setting up your grades view to minimize scrolling

The **Enter Grades** page displays all of your course's grade items and student scores in a long, scrolling table. While it's incredibly useful to have all of the grades for a single course at your fingertips, the amount of information on the screen can make the interface too cluttered and distracting, if you aren't careful. Fortunately, you can adjust the tool's display settings to customize your view and eliminate any unnecessary information.

Getting ready

In order to complete this recipe, you're going to need to have access to a D2L course with a completed grade book and at least a few enrolled students.

How to do it...

In this brief recipe, we'll look at how you can use the Grade tool's personal display options to minimize scrolling.

1. Access your course and navigate to the **Grades** tool.
2. Click on the **Settings** link in the upper-right corner of the **Enter Grades** page.

3. By default, student names are repeated after every fifth grade column. Depending on your monitor's resolution, this may be too often or not often enough. If your resolution is relatively high, you may want to change the **Number of columns before user details repeat** text field from **5** to a larger number such as 8 or 10. You may need to experiment to find a number that works best with your display.

4. By default, the names of grade item columns are repeated after every 15 students. Change the number in the **Number of users before column header repeats** text field to optimize this setting for your display:

* Number of columns before user details repeat: 8

* Number of users before column header repeats: 20

5. Click on the **Save** button.

How it works...

One way of minimizing scrolling is to modify the frequency at which student names and grade item titles appear in the grades table. The Grade tool's default settings seem to work best for low-resolution displays. Larger monitors, or those with a higher resolution, are capable of displaying more information on screen at a given time. If you're using such a display, there's a good chance you can increase the number of columns between the user details and also the number of rows between repeated grade item names. You should experiment with different intervals to find a setting that works best for you.

There's more...

Another easy way of reducing horizontal scrolling is to hide future grade items, or even past grade items you no longer need to see, in the **Enter Grades** screen. You can do this by clicking on the **Settings** link in the top-right corner of the grade list and unchecking the checkboxes next to any item you no longer wish to see. The student view is unaffected by the options you specify here, and you can easily access the **Settings** area any time if you need to view the hidden grade columns.

See also

▶ The *Previewing grades from a student's perspective* recipe

Creating a new letter grade scheme

Grade schemes are used to help identify the levels of student achievement in the Grade tool. Some common schemes include percentages and letter grades, but you can even create your own value scale or point schemes. Although your system administrators may have defined some common grade schemes for your institution, you can create or modify existing schemes to match your grading policy. In this recipe, we will create a new letter grade scheme from scratch.

Getting ready

We will be working with a simplified grade scheme in the following example. However, you'll find this recipe most useful if you modify the following steps to match your own syllabus.

How to do it...

In addition to creating a new grade scheme, we'll assign colors to each level of achievement in the scheme. This will make it easy to quickly assess students' performance levels when we view the **Enter Grades** page.

1. Access your course and navigate to the **Grades** tool.

2. Click on the **Schemes** link at the top of the page.

3. Click on the **New Scheme** button. Then, enter a name for the custom scheme in the **Name** text field.

4. We're going to create a standard A to F grade scheme. Starting in the first row, enter the letter F and work your way up through the other letter grades. By default, the system only creates three rows, so type 2 in the **Add Ranges** text field and click on the **Add Ranges** link.

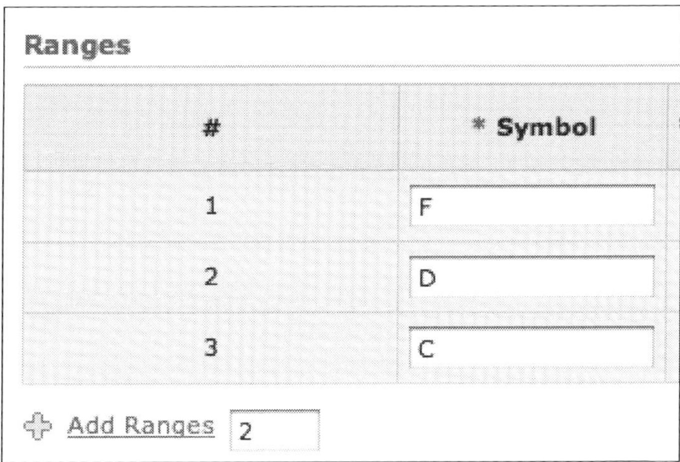

5. Let's go ahead and fill in the percentages for each grade range. For each row, we will type the lowest possible percentage required to earn each letter grade. For example, students earning **59.5** will earn **D** in the following scheme.

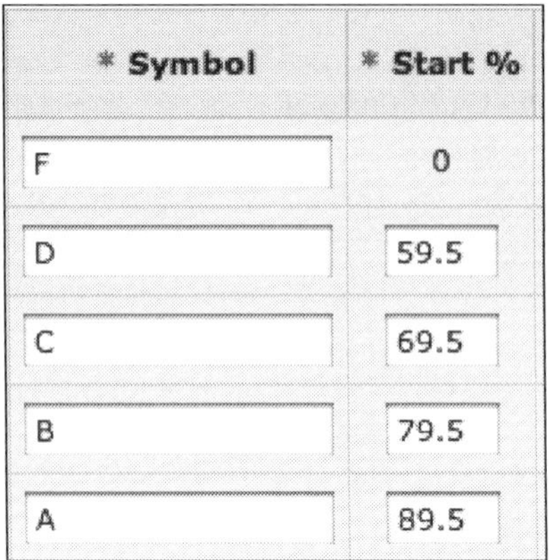

* Symbol	* Start %
F	0
D	59.5
C	69.5
B	79.5
A	89.5

6. We can also assign a color for each range, so that we can get a good indication of how students are doing in class as soon as we access the Grades tool. Click on the small triangle in the color column and choose a new color for each row.

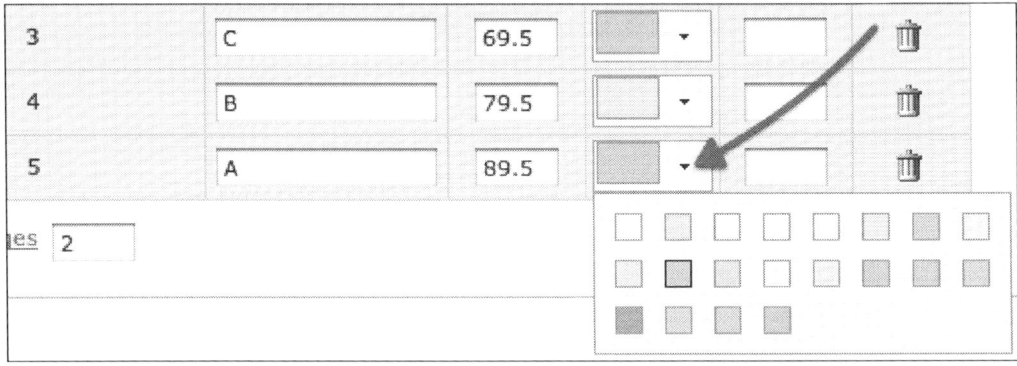

7. Save your new scheme by clicking on the **Save** button.

8. Now that we have a custom grade scheme, let's make it the default for all grade items in our course. Find your new grade scheme at the bottom of the list. Click on the checkmark icon to activate the scheme as the default scheme for the course. Click on the **Yes** button in the **Confirmation** pop-up window.

How it works...

We began this recipe by creating a new, empty grade scheme. However, you can also copy and modify an existing scheme if you need something that's relatively similar to an existing one. The **Copy** option can be found by clicking on the **More Actions** button on the **Schemes** page.

After creating a new scheme and naming it, fill in the **Symbols** column with values. Since we're creating a letter grade scheme in this tutorial, we chose to enter the letters A to F, but you could put anything you'd like here: `Does not meet expectations, Exceeds Expectations`, and so on. Next, fill in the required information for the **Start %** column. You'll want to start at **0%** and work our way up the grade scheme. Make sure that you enter the lowest possible score for each symbol. Although optional, we assigned a color to each level of our scheme in step 6. This can help give both, the instructors and students, a quick indication of performance on each assignment.

There's more...

After creating and assigning a custom grade scheme, we still need to visit the **Grades Settings** area to make sure that the scheme is set to appear in both the instructor and student views.

1. Click on the **Settings** link in the upper-right corner of the **Grades** tool.

2. To activate grade schemes for your view, visit the **Personal Display Options** tab and make sure the **Grade scheme symbol** and **Grade scheme color** options are selected.

3. Let's go ahead and turn on grade schemes for students as well. While still in the **Grades Settings** area, click on the **Org Unit Display Options** link and verify that both the **Grade scheme symbol** and **Grade scheme color** options are checked under the **Submission view Display Options** header.

4. Click on the **Save** button when finished.

See also

 ► The *Previewing grades from a student's perspective* recipe

Calculating and releasing final grades

Unless you otherwise specify in the **Restrictions** tab, students can typically view grade book scores as soon as you enter them into the system. Final grades, however, are handled differently. You need to calculate and release final grades before students can view them.

Getting ready

You'll need a course with a completed grade book in order to complete this recipe. Please note that your institution may have additional requirements for releasing final grades, such as transferring scores to a student information system, so make sure to view your school's documentation as well.

How to do it...

In this recipe, we'll learn how to calculate and release final grades for all students in a course.

1. Access your course and navigate to the **Grades** tool.

2. Let's check a couple of settings before we calculate and release the final grades. Click on the **Grades Settings** link and visit the **Calculation Options** tab.

3. Make sure the options to release **Adjusted Final Grade** and **Treat ungraded items as 0** are selected, as shown in the following screenshot:

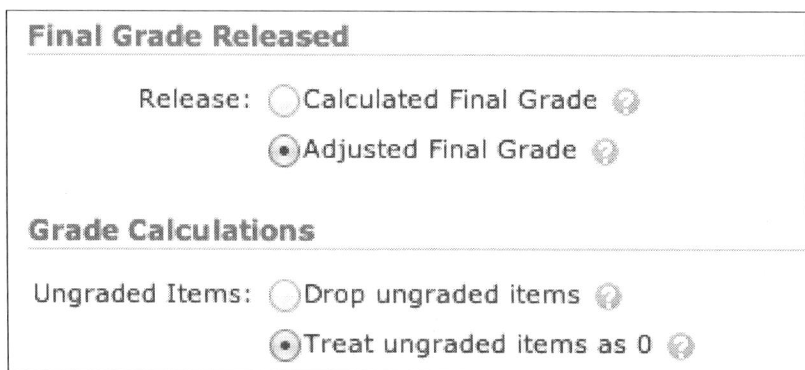

4. Click on the **Save** button, then click on the **Yes** button when prompted.

5. Click on the **Close** button and navigate to the **Manage Grades** tab.

6. Click on the **Final Adjusted Grade** link. Let's provide a new name for the grade item by typing one in the **Name** text field. I'm going to call mine **Course Grade**, but name yours whatever you'd like.

7. Make sure that the correct scheme is selected in the **Grade Scheme** drop-down menu. Take a look at the previous recipe for information on creating your own **Grade Schemes**.

8. Let's show the students both the class average and the distribution of grades, by selecting the appropriate options under the **Display Options** heading:

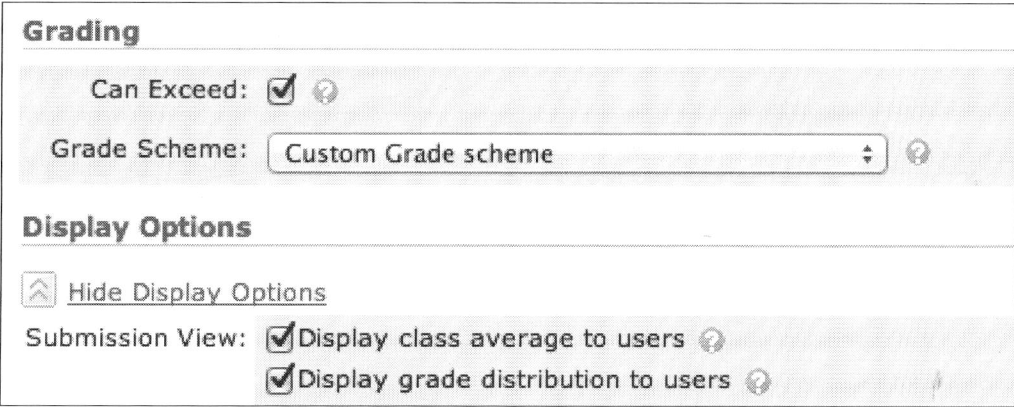

9. Click on the **Save and Close** button.

10. We can now release the final grades to students. From the **Manage Grades** tab, activate the context menu for the **Final Adjusted Grade** item and select the **Enter Grades** option:

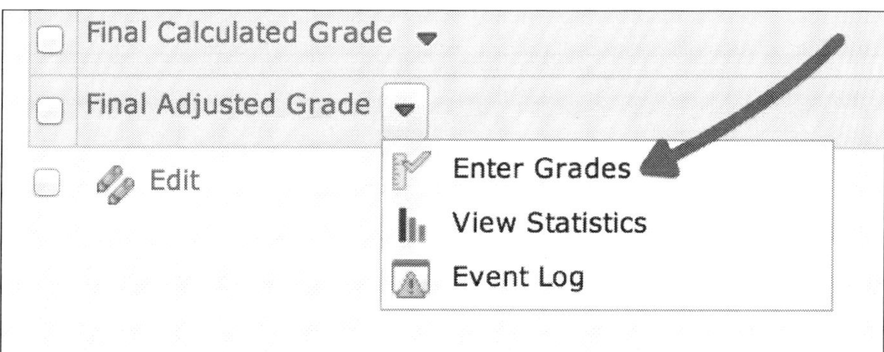

11. Let's make sure all of the grades are up-to-date by clicking on the **Recalculate All** option in the **Final Grades** context menu:

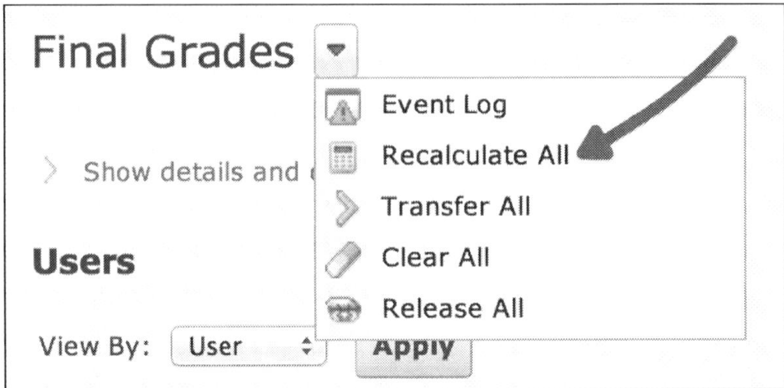

12. Select the **Final Calculated Grade** option and click on the **Calculate** button. Click on the **Calculate** button again when prompted. Finally, click on the **Yes** button.

13. Now, we can transfer the calculated total to the **Final Adjusted Grade** column by clicking on the **Transfer All** option in the **Final Grades** context menu. Click on the **Yes** button when prompted. Click on the **Yes** button a final time to complete the process.

14. In order for students to see their final grades, we need to release it to them. Let's choose the **Release All** option in the same context menu to release grades for all students on our class. Click on the **Yes** button when prompted.

How it works...

In this recipe, we chose to release a final adjusted grade to students in our class. Selecting this option allows us to modify the final grades generated by the system, before releasing them to students. While you probably won't need to adjust these scores often, it's usually a good idea to leave the option open. We also checked the option to treat ungraded items as 0. This means that students earning zeroes on assignments for which there is no score recorded in the system. Without checking this option, ungraded assignments don't count against students. Next, we visited the **Manage Grades** area and changed the name of the **Adjusted Final Grade** column to something a little more meaningful.

After verifying the settings in the **Manage Grades** tab, it's time to calculate and release the final grades to the students. Begin by clicking on the **Recalculate All** option to make sure that all of the final calculated scores are up-to-date. Then, transfer the calculated scores to the adjusted column using the **Transfer All** option. Notice that both the **points earned** and **total possible points** fields in the **Final Adjusted Grade** column are editable. You can increase the number of points in the numerator text field to account for any extra credit a student may have earned (that's not already been entered into the grade book). Finally, we clicked on the **Release All** option to make the final grades visible to the students. The checkboxes in the **Release Final Adjusted** Grade column indicates that the grade has been released to the students:

See also

> ▸ The *Creating a new letter grade scheme* and *Exporting a backup copy of your grades* recipes

Previewing grades from a student's perspective

The Learning Environment's grade book is extremely customizable. We can alter the look and feel of both, the student and instructor views of the tool, by adjusting settings in several areas. Since the tool is so easily customizable, your view of the tools will often be very different from the view your students see. In this recipe, we'll learn how to view the tool from the student perspective, which can be especially helpful when questions about grades arise. Although you can examine some aspects of the student view using the **Role Switch** widget, we'll be using the **Preview** button in the **Enter Grades** area because it allows us to view not only the user interface but also the student's scores.

Getting ready

You will need access to a course with at least one enrolled student in order to complete this recipe.

How to do it...

In the following steps, we will learn how to use the **Preview** button in the **Grades** tool.

1. Access your course and navigate to the **Grades** tool.

2. Click on the name of a student in the **Grades** list. This will display all grades for a particular student in your course.

3. Click on the **Preview** link in the user context menu at the top of the page.

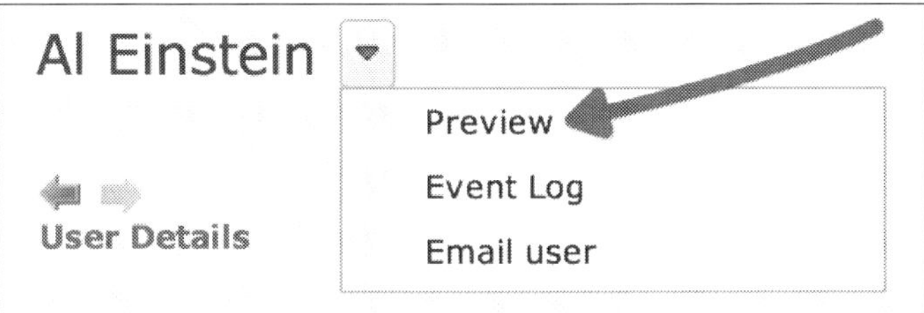

4. Make sure everything looks the way you expect. Then, click on the **Close** button when finished.

How it works...

The steps in this recipe are very straightforward. After navigating to the **Enter Grades** area, we clicked on the name of a student whose grades we want to view. The **Preview** button in the context menu allows us to see the grade book for a specific student.

See also

▸ The *Hiding grade items from students* recipe

Viewing grades for students who have withdrawn from a course

When students withdraw or are un-enrolled from a Desire2Learn Learning Suite course, all of their work and grades are typically hidden from the instructor view. However, this information is still stored within the database in case you need to access it again in the future. In this recipe, we'll learn how to view the grades and progress of a student who is no longer enrolled in your course. This information can be useful for grade appeals or when students transfer to another section of the same course.

Getting ready

In order to complete this recipe, you'll need the instructor access to a course that at least one student who has dropped.

How to do it...

The following steps explain how to use reports in the **Grades** tool to track the progress of students who are no longer enrolled in the course.

1. Access your course and navigate to the **Classlist** tool.

2. Click on the **Enrollment Statistics** button at the top of the page.

3. Beneath the summary table of enrollments, you'll find a **Withdrawals** heading with a table containing the names of each student that has withdrawn from the course. Locate the name of the student, activate the context menu, and select the **View grades** option

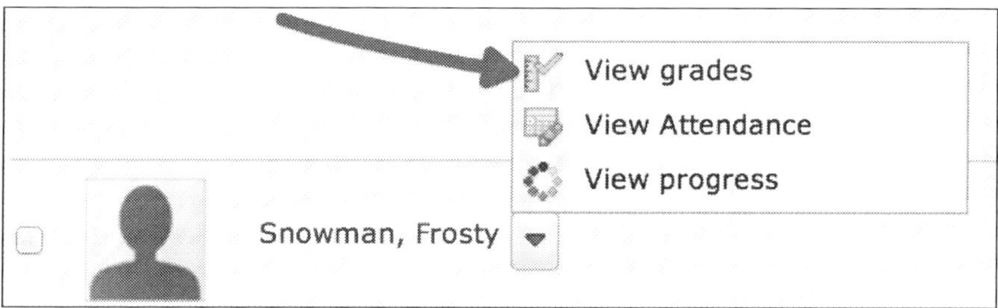

4. You'll see a detailed list of all of the selected student's grades. When finished, go ahead and click on the **Cancel** button to return to the **Enrollment Statistics** area.

How it works...

While it might seem logical to visit the grade book to locate this information, you'll need to visit the **Classlist** tool instead. Once there, use the **Report** button to navigate to a list of current enrollments and withdrawals. Clicking on the **View** grades option for a student in the **Withdrawals** section displays that student's scores.

Exporting a backup copy of your grades

Although the Desire2Learn Learning Suite uses safeguards to protect against data loss, it's always a good idea to backup important information such as student grades. In this recipe, we will learn how to export the contents of your online grade book to a downloadable CSV file. In addition to serving as a backup, you can also access and modify the information in this file using any standard spreadsheet authoring program, such as Microsoft Excel, Apple's Numbers app, and Open Office.

Getting ready

You'll need a course with a complete grade book and at least one student in order to complete this recipe.

How to do it...

In the following steps, we will customize and export a backup copy of your online grade book.

1. Access your course and navigate to the **Grades** tool. If you aren't taken to the **Enter Grades** area automatically, go ahead and click on the **Enter Grades** link at the top of the page.

2. Click on the **Export** button at the top of the page.

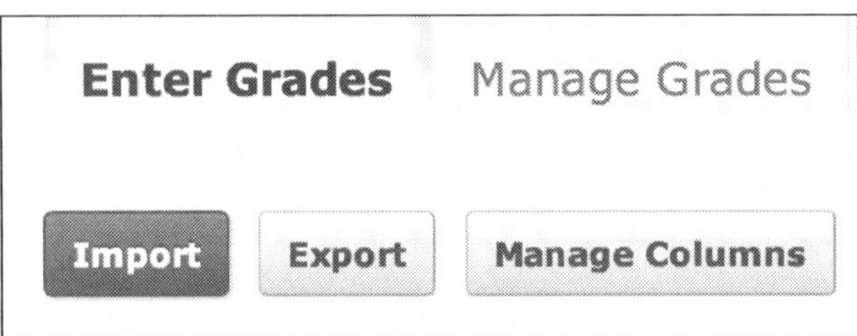

3. Let's make sure we have all of the information we need in our grades export. Make sure that both options are checked in the **Grade Values** section and select the **First Name** and **Last Name** options under the **User Details** section:

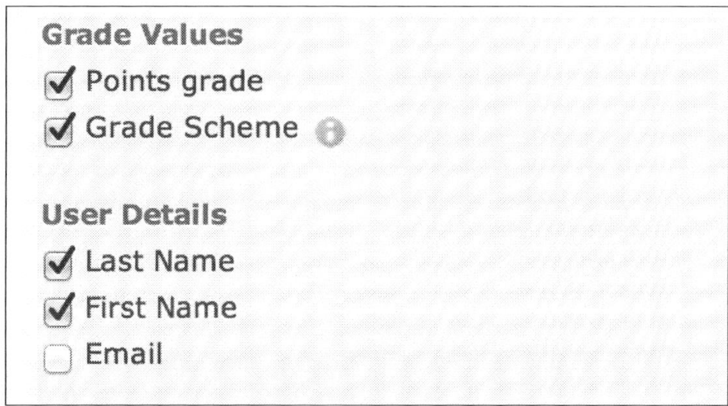

4. In the **Choose Grades to Export** section, select the checkboxes next to each item you want to include in the backup file. You can select everything using the checkbox in the table header.

5. Click on the **Export to CSV** button.

6. Once available, click on the link to download the file.

7. Click on the **Close** button to dismiss the pop-up window.

8. Once the CSV file has been downloaded to your computer, you can open it using Microsoft Excel, Apple's Numbers, Open Office, or just about any spreadsheet application.

How it works...

By default, the system's export file only includes **Org Defined ID** of a student. In order to make the file easier to use later on, we also selected the options to include the students' first and last names. This will make the file much more readable if you ever need to access it. We also selected the checkboxes next to each grade item that we want to include in the export before clicking on the **Export to CSV** button. Once your file is processed, you can download it to your computer by clicking on the name of the file.

Index

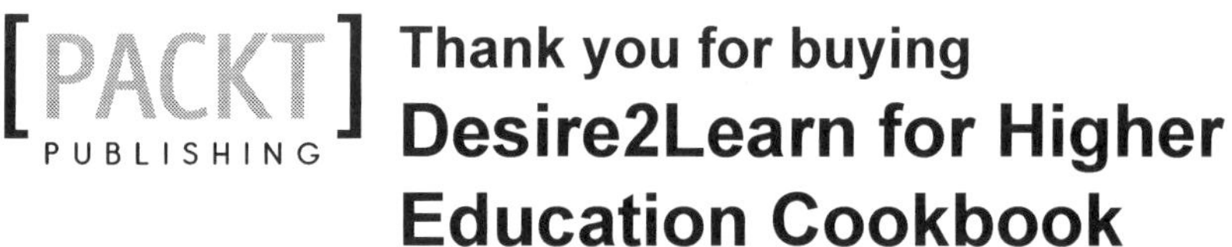

About Packt Publishing

Packt, pronounced 'packed', published its first book "*Mastering phpMyAdmin for Effective MySQL Management*" in April 2004 and subsequently continued to specialize in publishing highly focused books on specific technologies and solutions.

Our books and publications share the experiences of your fellow IT professionals in adapting and customizing today's systems, applications, and frameworks. Our solution based books give you the knowledge and power to customize the software and technologies you're using to get the job done. Packt books are more specific and less general than the IT books you have seen in the past. Our unique business model allows us to bring you more focused information, giving you more of what you need to know, and less of what you don't.

Packt is a modern, yet unique publishing company, which focuses on producing quality, cutting-edge books for communities of developers, administrators, and newbies alike. For more information, please visit our website: `www.packtpub.com`.

Writing for Packt

We welcome all inquiries from people who are interested in authoring. Book proposals should be sent to `author@packtpub.com`. If your book idea is still at an early stage and you would like to discuss it first before writing a formal book proposal, contact us; one of our commissioning editors will get in touch with you.

We're not just looking for published authors; if you have strong technical skills but no writing experience, our experienced editors can help you develop a writing career, or simply get some additional reward for your expertise.

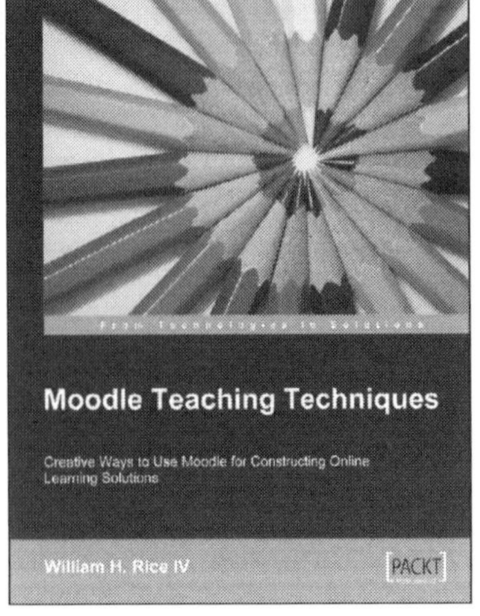

Moodle Teaching Techniques

ISBN: 978-1-847192-84-4   Paperback: 192 pages

Create Ways to Use Moodle for Constructing Online Learning Solutions

1. Applying your teaching techniques through Moodle

2. Creative uses for Moodle's standard features

3. Workarounds, providing alternative solutions

4. Abundantly illustrated with screenshots of the solutions you'll build

5. When and how to apply the different learning solutions

6. Especially good for university and professional teachers

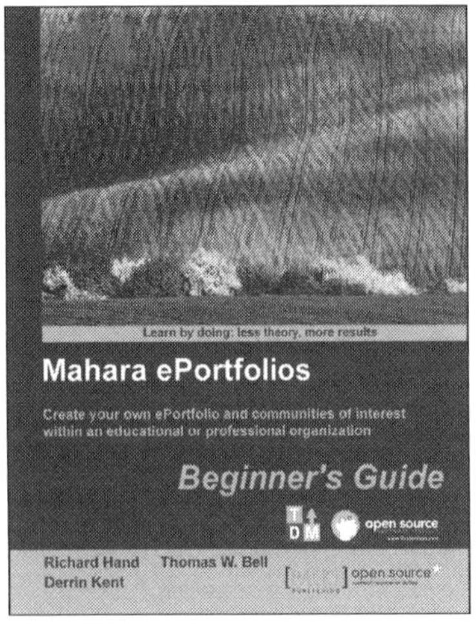

Mahara ePortfolios: Beginner's Guide

ISBN: 978-1-849517-76-8   Paperback: 328 pages

Create your own ePortfolio and communities of interest within an educational or professional organization

1. A step-by-step approach that takes you through examples with ample screenshots and clear explanations

2. Create, customize, and maintain an impressive personal digital portfolio of web pages and mini websites (collections) with a simple point-and-click interface

3. Create and manage online learning communities and social networks through groups, shared file areas, and forums

Please check **www.PacktPub.com** for information on our titles